HOW TO FIND A JOB AS A PARALEGAL

A Step-by-Step Job Search Guide

Second Edition

Marie Kisiel, Ph.D.
Roosevelt University

West Publishing Company
St. Paul   New York   Los Angeles   San Francisco

Copyediting and production: Publication Support Services
Design: Michael J. Sweeney
Cover: Michael J. Sweeeney

Copyright © 1989   By CARRUS BOOKS
Copyright © 1992   By WEST PUBLISHING COMPANY
                     50 W. Kellogg Boulevard
                     P.O. Box 64526
                     St. Paul, MN 55164-0526

Printed in the United States of America

99 98 97 96 95 94 93 92   8 7 6 5 4 3 2 1 0

Library of Congress Cataloging-in-Publication Data

Kisiel, Marie.
    How to find a job as a paralegal: a step-by-step search guide /
  Marie Kisiel, 2nd ed.
        p. cm.

    Includes index.
    1. Legal assistants—Vocational guidance—United States. 2. Job hunting—United States.
I. Title
KF320.L4K57   1991   340'.023'73--dc20
ISBN 0-314-92053-6 (soft)   91-26345
                                        ∞   CIP

HOW TO FIND A JOB AS A PARALEGAL

A Step-by-Step Job Search Guide

Second Edition

Acknowledgements

I am particularly grateful to Jean Hellman, Director of the Institute for Paralegal Studies at Loyola University, for her ongoing encouragement and thorough editorial comments; to Adrienne Hochstadt, Cassandra Kisiel, and Phillip Exel for their insights and evaluations; and especially to Linda Demkowicz for her diligent professional work and creative suggestions in the final preparation of the manuscript. Their loyal support as colleagues and as friends is very important to me.

I would like to acknowledge the American Bar Association, Standing Committee on Legal Assistants, for their permission to reprint the legal assistant definition from *The ABA Guidelines and Procedures for Obtaining ABA Approval of Legal Education Programs*.

In addition, the following people read the manuscript and offered many valuable suggestions for improvement: Delores Grissom, Samford University; Betsy O'Neil Covington, Denver Paralegal Institute; Susan Stoner, Southeastern Paralegal Institute; Susan H. Brewer, J. Sargeant Reynolds Community College; Barbara Quigley, Balin Institute; Therese A. Cannon, University of West Los Angeles; and George Schrader, Auburn University at Montgomery.

Finally, my thanks to the Lawyer's Assistant Program of Roosevelt University in Chicago. While Director of Pre-Employment, I developed the first edition of this book which was adopted as a workshop manual.

How to Use This Book

This book is designed for the paralegal embarking on the strenuous, challenging task of finding a job. It is a step-by-step guide to understanding the responsibilities of becoming a paralegal and developing the skills to find the right position in this fast-growing profession.

Depending upon your background, experience, and/or specific problems in starting out as a paralegal, you may wish to focus on specific chapters. In order to gain the maximum benefit from this book, however, you should at least review each step before going on to the following one.

How to Find a Job as a Paralegal should serve as a job source guide, a professional primer, and a workbook. Use it to help you understand yourself and what you have to offer the paralegal profession.

Remember that getting a job is a skill in itself and the person who is best prepared for that task is the one who will have the greatest success. May this book help you to achieve that goal.

Contents

HOW TO FIND A JOB AS A PARALEGAL

A Step-by-Step Job Search Guide

Second Edition

Introduction

According to the Bureau of Labor Statistics (*Occupational Outlook Handbook*, 1990-91), paralegals will continue to be the fastest growing profession of the next decade. One reason for the growth may be that some organizations are now offering paralegals a career track. With added training and responsibilities, they become even more cost-efficient. The best positions, of course, will be highly competitive, but prospects for the profession are bright.

Who are paralegals? What do they do? Why have they become so sought after? And, most important, how do they find employment once they have had the necessary training?

You will find the answers in this book.

These answers will not be simple because people from all types of back-grounds, experiences, and credentials are entering the field. This includes students with little or no professional experience in any field, legal secretaries, career changers — including former teachers, salespeople, artists, insurance and realty experts, and on and on. These are the people who are attracted to the field for many reasons.

The profession offers extensive opportunities for those with broad experiences and backgrounds; however, the field takes a special type of person. Lawyers and law firms are looking for candidates with strong organizational skills; effective communicators; people who can write and speak and are detail-oriented and, above all, flexible — in their tasks and frequently, in their schedules.

This book will help you to focus your skills and strengths and help you to become the best *employed* paralegal you can be. It will serve as a step-by-step guide to help you to understand the role of the paralegal and develop a job search plan that will enable you to achieve that goal.

You will learn how to identify what you have to offer: your unique talents, skills, and achievements that you have developed, *whatever* your background.

Step One, Self-Assessment, will enable you to recognize what you have achieved and what you have to offer an employer. Through a comprehensive self-inventory, you will learn how to analyze your past experiences so that you can focus on them in a resumé. You will also be shown how to highlight the specific accomplishments of your academic background and how to use various part-time or volunteer work experiences as part of your professional record.

Exercises and chronological charts are included to help you recognize what you have achieved in addition to your paralegal training. Inasmuch as your backgrounds will be varied, the results will vary. The important point, however, is for you to identify your own unique skills and accomplishments, whatever your background. As you do this, you will be setting the groundwork for writing a resumé that is the best reflection of you, where you have been, and what you have done. It is essential groundwork and well worth the effort you will invest.

Step Two of the job search plan is the resumé: your professional profile. While there is no one *right* way to write a resumé, you will need to develop a resumé that works for you. The purpose of the resumé is *not* to get you the job; it is to get you the interview. Your self-assessment will prepare you for what you are to include on your resumé as a paralegal. In the resumé chapter various formats are discussed to help you to choose the best one for you. This chapter explains the various categories to be included and the variety of options you have in presenting the information about yourself on the resumé, without cluttering the page with needless details.

"Problem areas" are also discussed in this section: how to account for long gaps in employment, the wide variety of jobs you may have held, diverse backgrounds, limited work experience, and so forth.

How do you let the employer see your best profile without unethical padding or falsifying information? If you have done a thorough job at the first stage, you can usually find more pertinent information that you may have thought of earlier in your job search plan.

In addition to the content and format material, this section also addresses the very important issue of the physical appearance of your resumé. Suggestions on paper weight and color, spacing, headings, printing vs. professional typing, and so forth will be offered.

At the end of this section, sample resumés representing a wide range of backgrounds and experiences are included.

Step Three of your job search discusses the cover letter and its importance: how to individualize your letter and how to make it relevant to the resumé you have just completed, *and* how to tailor this letter to the job for which you are applying.

The cover letter will be your introduction on paper. It should make a potential employer take a closer look at your resumé and want to meet you. Several model cover letters in this section illustrate how you can focus on your specific skills, talents, and achievements in a short letter. In addition to sample cover letters, follow-up letters are included in this section: letters to send after you have had the interview, letters that will reinforce the positive impression you wish to make.

Step Four of your job search will be the most crucial step of all: the interview. The interview will also be the most stressful step. How well you are prepared will frequently determine how successful you are at this stage of your job search. All of the work you have done so far is preparatory for this final step. This section discusses how to handle this most important, and frequently most difficult, part of your job search.

Included in this discussion is a list of do's and don'ts in the interview. You will also find steps that you can take to prepare yourself, including typical interview questions and how you can rehearse yourself to answer such questions. In addition, there is a list of questions you should ask and guidelines on information you should already know about the position and the organization.

The legalities of interviewing are discussed in this section — questions which cannot be asked legally, but what to do if they are asked.

How do you negotiate a salary? How do you know when the interview is over? How can you evaluate your interview performance so you can improve your interviewing style? And what do you do next?

All of these questions are addressed in this valuable section.

The Appendix of this book is your information guide. This final section provides you with a list of resources and a job notebook — as well as directions on how to use them most profitably.

These resources include: law lists, insurance companies, paralegal associations, directories and periodicals such as *Martindale-Hubbell, Standard and Poor's, The American Lawyer Guide*, and others.

For those thinking about free-lancing as a paralegal, a brief section will be included on how to proceed once you have made a decision to create your own job. This section also includes a discussion of how you can use your job as a paralegal as a stepping stone to other careers.

Remember that as you read each section, you will have to adapt the information to your own needs and your own set of individual circumstances. The job search plan is a guide for you. While each section can be read separately, apart from other sections, you will gain the maximum benefit from mastering each step before going on to the following one. If you are encountering problems, go back and review the points included. Try not to hurry through. The time and effort you invest in developing a successful job campaign will result in your finding the job you really want and deserve!

What Is a Paralegal and Why Is the Paralegal Profession Growing?

2

A paralegal, also known as a legal assistant, is a non-lawyer who assists attorneys in their professional legal duties. While education and training enhances a person's ability to get a job, there is no required certification to become a paralegal; there is no licensing or compulsory examination.

Perhaps the best way to describe a paralegal is to explain some of the many tasks paralegals perform.

According to the American Bar Association, *Standing Committee on Legal Assistants* (*ABA Guidelines and Procedures for Obtaining ABA Approval of Legal Assistant Education Programs*, ABA, 1987, 1989, 1990):

> A legal assistant is a person, qualified through education, training, or work experience, who is employed or retained by a lawyer, law office, governmental agency, or other entity in a capacity or function which involves the performance, under the ultimate direction and supervision of an attorney, of specifically delegated substantive legal work, which work, for the most part, requires a sufficient knowledge of legal concepts that, absent such assistant, the attorney would perform the task.

These are, of course, only some of the duties which paralegals perform. Many are involved in almost every aspect of a lawyer's work, except representing clients in court or giving legal advice.

Paralegals do legal research, draft briefs, interview witnesses, assist at trials, file legal documents, handle real estate closings, label documents, or perhaps even photocopy materials. The range of work is wide; the use of a person's talents is variable, depending on the job that needs to be done. It can be exciting; it can be tedious. It is always important.

That is why paralegals are so much in demand. The work they do is essential to a lawyer. It is the time-consuming detail work that would frequently be too costly for a lawyer to perform; yet, without an efficient, reliable assistant, lawyers often cannot do their jobs. The greatest hiring argument for paralegals, therefore, is cost-effectiveness. Legal cases are frequently so complex that it is impossible for one attorney to be a specialist in every area. Most large law firms are broken down into specialty departments: real estate, litigation, corporate finance, etc. If an attorney chooses one specialty, it stands to reason he or she will need a specialized paralegal for assistance.

Today, it is not unusual for a large law firm to have over 100 lawyers on staff; many have branch offices all over the world. With expanded services and the growth of increasingly complex legal regulations, these firms continue to demand skilled paralegals. In order to meet this need, some organizations are now moving towards a tier system for paralegals, a trend discussed in *Legal Assistant Today* (March/April 1991). This system offers paralegals an opportunity to move up the career ladder by assuming new tasks and responsibilities. Higher ranking means higher pay for these paralegals.

Of course, not all of these paralegals will choose to work in a large, often fast-paced, legal environment. Many will prefer the setting of a social agency or smaller legal office. The person with generalist training is prepared to handle a variety of tasks — and that may be more appealing. Later on in this book, we also discuss some guidelines, as well as employment opportunities, for those who wish to free-lance as a paralegal.

Whatever the setting, the qualifications — both personal and professional — are similar. The amount of experience and training necessary varies, depending upon the competition in a current job market, as well as the specific position. Basically, however, a thorough, intensive paralegal training program is excellent preparation for an entry-level position. Learning on the job provides the additional training that is essential for any given position.

The personal characteristics which are requisite for any position are equally important. In addition to those qualities which are the earmarks of a successful candidate for any job in any field — reliability, commitment, diligence, etc. — the successful paralegal will have the competitive edge if he or she has strongly developed communication skills, both written and oral, as well as interpersonal communication. Working with clients, handling research, getting along with a wide variety of personality types, frequently under stressful conditions — demands those qualities that cannot be learned in a classroom. They are the characteristics which lawyers look for when selecting the best paralegal for the position.

Other skills that may have been developed in other jobs, whatever the field, can enhance a paralegal's opportunity to get the position and perform effectively on the job. Think of the knowledge and expertise you have gained through your college education, if you have a degree or have attended college. A major or minor in any field may be the source of valuable, relevant skills that could make you an asset. If you do not have a college education, any work skills you have developed, including business skills, organizational skills, computer skills, foreign language skills — all these and more may prove to be an asset to a firm or particular attorney. *Every* position presents an opportunity for someone to develop specific skills as well as accomplishments.

In the next chapter, you will discover those skills, interests, and talents you have developed, along with your achievements. Once you discover your assets, you can convey them to a potential employer.

Self-assessment or self-inventory is an essential part of the job search. You must begin there so that you can focus on those skills in a resumé. But in order to do that, you need to take the time to look at yourself, see where you have been and where you want to go as a paralegal.

All of this preparation will help you to prepare for the final stage: interviewing for the job. When a potential employer asks you to "tell me something about yourself," you will be prepared to answer, for by that time you will have thought about it carefully.

You will also be able to understand what there is about *you* that will make a good paralegal. By understanding how you are *personally* prepared to do that job, you are getting ready to face your job campaign with all the tools and information you need.

So let's start at the beginning of the process: with you.

Preliminary Self-Assess-ment Exercise

Before you begin your self-assessment and self-inventory in the following chapter, write a brief statement below about *why* you want to become a paralegal and why you think you are qualified.

Remember that this is a preliminary exercise. Nevertheless, you will be starting to think of yourself as a professional, in very specific ways. When you have completed this book, you may wish to return to this exercise to see how much you have learned about yourself in the pages that follow.

Why I would like to become a paralegal and why I think I am qualified:

_____

_____

_____

_____

_____

_____

_____

_____

_____

_____

_____

_____

_____

_____

_____

_____

_____

_____

Self-Assessment/ Self-Inventory

3

The purpose of a self-assessment, which is frequently referred to as a self-inventory, is to help you focus on your qualifications, skills, and achievements so that you can best present them to a potential employer in a resumé. In order to do this, however, you must carefully review all of the activities in which you have participated and all of the jobs you have held (part-time, full-time, paid or volunteer). Go back as far as you like, or as far as you can recall a job that seems to have offered you an opportunity to develop *specific skills* or achieve *noteworthy accomplishments*.

The charts you are about to complete will be useful as a part of your resumé preparation. They will give you a broad view of your accomplishments as they relate to the work you have done, even though they do not represent your current field of interest.

List *all* the jobs you have held, even if the specific job was unpaid, the place of employment, your title, duties, and accomplishments. Begin with the most recent year you worked or held a job and list backwards, year by year, to the earliest job you can remember in which you developed any skills. At this point, don't be concerned with repetitious lines. Later on, you can edit the list if you wish.

In the Accomplishments column, describe what you feel are your most significant accomplishments or contributions to your job. These accomplishments should relate to specific areas, if possible, such as increased efficiency, better designs, higher sales or profits, improved human relations, better working conditions, new or improved programs, and happier or healthier work environments.

After a review, you may wish to add to this chart later on. At this point, try to get down as much information about yourself as you remember.

Work Chronology

Year	Organization	Title	Duties / Activities	Skills / Accomplishments

Now that you have chronicled your activities, what you have enjoyed doing and seem to be doing consistently, either on a job or as an outside interest, let's examine how your achievements or accomplishments are related to what you enjoy doing and identify the network of specific skills you have developed over the years.

On the following pages, you are asked to identify your skills. After reviewing your chronology chart, you should have a fresh idea of what you did in your previous jobs and activities. Now you are given the opportunity to focus on these skills again as an essential part of your resumé preparation, and indicate the degree of competence you feel that you have achieved. Although you may find some overlapping, you will discover trends and patterns in your life, along with specific skills.

Analyzing Your Accomplishments and Evaluating Your Skills

Skills Inventory

Skill	Excellent	Very Good	Good	Fair	Skill	Excellent	Very Good	Good	Fair
Analyzing					Problem-solving				
Budgeting					Persuading				
Building					Policy-making				
Computer Skills					Promoting				
Specific Programs:					Researching				
					Repairing				
					Selling				
Coordinating					Shorthand				
Counseling					Supervising				
Creating					Speaking				
Decision-making					Teaching				
Designing					Training				
Directing					Troubleshooting				
Drafting					Typing				
Editing					Writing				
Inventing					Others:				
Languages (specify)									
Leading									
Listening									
Managing									
Meeting Planning									
Motivating									
Negotiating									
Observing									
Organizing									
Performing									
Planning									
Presenting									

After completing your work chronology and skills inventory, you will probably realize that skills do not exist in isolation. Any one skill involves a whole series of related and transferable skills. And if you can realize how the things you do well are generally related to what you enjoy doing, then you have reached a very important stage in thinking about your career.

Here are some examples of how you can achieve such a realization.

Perhaps you are happiest when you work with people you know, but you are not comfortable with strangers. Perhaps you are happiest when you work alone. You may dislike the work, but love solving problems, financial or personal. Or you may relish situations in which you can be the organizer or person in charge. You may enjoy building a boat or cooking a gourmet meal, but not enjoy following a specified set of instructions. What should become obvious to you is what makes you happy while you are working or playing.

Common threads may not be apparent and sometimes it is easier to work with someone — a spouse or friend — who can help you recognize the skills you have developed or that are transferable. Such an exercise can be extremely beneficial as you prepare your resumé or your job interview.

Anything from organizing a car pool to managing an office demonstrates a special skill. Skills required for a job are more valued than those used in a hobby, homemaking, or volunteer work, but *they may be the same skills.* A chairperson for a charity fund-raising drive has acquired skills in planning, organizing, delegating, bookkeeping, and communicating, as well as many others. A president of the Parents' Club at the local high school needs to develop skills in motivating others, promoting and publicizing, negotiating, writing and speaking, and dealing with people.

Almost anything you have done can be broken down into a series of steps and analyzed in terms of functions and skills. For example: you do volunteer work for a teenage rehabilitation center on weekends. You recognize that some of the teenagers have severe reading problems. You begin to read aloud to individual young people on a one-on-one basis, pronouncing and explaining the meaning of each word. What are you doing? You think you are helping a youngster, and you are, but let's analyze the situation a little more closely.

Problem: Difficulty in reading

Reason: Youngster's lack of concentration, inability to recognize, understand, and pronounce words.

Solution: Confidence-building, understanding of youngster's social/emotional environment. Patient, supervised practice. Continued support as youngster improves.

Once the situation is described, it becomes easier to identify skills you developed and used, skills which may not be obvious at first glance. The help you give to the youngster in the above situation involves the use of very specific skills. In addition to helping the youngster to overcome a reading problem, which in itself demonstrates an ability to perceive the core of the problem and to offer a solution, you have demonstrated patience, understanding, and strong motivational and communication skills.

Any woman who runs a large household or has moved nine times in seven years has undeniable skills! Although she may not list those activities on her resumé, she must recognize that she does have strong managerial skills and will then come to perceive herself as capable of far more than paid job experience on a resumé might otherwise indicate. Anyone who works on a school committee may have developed skills in buying, selling, motivating, negotiating, communicating, and many others. A successful fund-raiser has a business sense, an eye for detail and accuracy — plus a proven track record. Specific figures, such as dollar amounts in budgets or percentage increases, are evidence that can and should be included on a resumé.

A similar problem faces recent college graduates who have limited job experiences, including seasonal positions such as waitressing, bartending, retail selling or clerical work.

How can you identify basic skills in these jobs without inflating their significance? Just think of those skills you have developed that would be useful in any profession and focus on them in your resumé.

For example:

Waitress, The Back Door Restaurant

- Worked varied shift schedules
- Supervised and trained temporary staff
- Handled cash receipts during vacation periods for regular cashier

Retail Sales Clerk, Morton's Department Store

- Handled all cash sales in three departments
- Assisted in annual stock inventory
- Participated in employees' staff development program

Bartender, Jeremy's Cafe

- Worked rotating day/evening shift
- Closed bar and balanced daily cash receipts
- Maintained inventory chart

The point here is that you cannot expect a potential employer to dig out these skills for you. You can do it once you recognize them. This is how the self-inventory charts can help you. Appreciate your past experiences and learn to articulate the skills you have found — both on your resumé and in an interview — rather than apologizing for what you think you have not done!

On a job application, in an interview, or even in casual conversation, never use the negative approach such as: "Although I do not have any specific experience in ...." Rather, focus on the skills you *have* developed in various settings that are appropriate and relevant to the job for which you are applying.

If you have been out of the job market or are entering an unrelated field, you must emphasize how you might have acquired strong skills in communication, management, interpersonal relations, or other areas from your past experience. Stress how these are skills that you strongly feel could be very useful in the particular position that is open.

When applying for a paralegal position, for example, focus on how your experience in *other* fields could prove to be an asset to you. Build on your achievements and experiences; make a potential employer recognize how much you have to offer — even though you have little or no experience in the position for which you are applying. You are more than qualified. Your job is to convince the person who will be hiring you. More strategies in "selling yourself" are discussed in a later chapter on interviewing.

When you realize all that you have achieved, your self-confidence will be greatly enhanced. Some of the gnawing questions will be answered: "I'm _____ years old and all I have done is teach . . . or keep house . . . or volunteer . . . or (fill in the blanks yourself), so who would want to hire me as a paralegal?"

When you begin to look at yourself in the most expansive way possible, it becomes easier to answer such questions in the most positive terms. That has been the purpose of this chapter on self-assessment.

Over these past few pages, you have been scrutinizing yourself, perhaps more carefully than you have ever done before. Doing so is essential if you are to successfully embark on your new career.

All of this self-discovery will lead to the results you want. You've taken a bold new step into a field which has required that you develop a new set of skills, but employers hire an entire person, not just a set of skills. What makes you valuable, both as a potential employee and human being, is your combination of interests and values, as well as skills. Yet before you can convince an employer that you are the best person for the job, you must have a fairly clear idea of what you can offer. You must be realistic and honest; but, at the same time, you must be able to present the best picture of yourself, including your strengths and achievements.

Throughout the past several pages you have been carefully and thoroughly scrutinizing yourself as a prospective employee. This has been some of the most important preliminary work of your job search, particularly as it relates to your resumé.

It has taken a great deal of probing and self-reflection to recognize what you have done. Now you are asked to review the information you have gathered about yourself and begin to find the phrases that capture what you have done. You may have already begun to choose and use some of these words that indicate the type of actions in which you were involved.

Words that describe your previous jobs, particularly job titles, may not be very helpful. However, words that convey accomplishment, involvement, or participation put your skills into focus. In analyzing your achievements, words or phrases such as: "I was responsible for ..." or "My duties involved..." do not convey what you actually did on the job.

A partial list of action words follows. It is important for you to be able to convey your own value to potential employers. Choosing the right words is essential if you are to convince them that you would be an asset. You may wish to use the following words or add to the list any words that are not included, but may be appropriate for you.

administered	drafted	invented	promoted
analyzed	edited	maintained	reduced costs
conducted	established	managed	researched
contracted	evaluated	operated	sold
created	exhibited	organized	supervised
designed	expended	planned	supported
developed	implemented	prepared	trained
directed	improved	produced	wrote

Review the list and now select those items which seem to represent those skills you have developed in your previous jobs. You may wish to review your earlier exercises to help you.

If you are still having a difficult time, examine the following entries which can serve as models for your own work achievement analysis. These examples can be expanded upon. Notice the use of action verbs, the avoidance of job descriptions, and the specific details used to quantify or demonstrate how the skill was achieved.

Job Experience (Paid or unpaid)	Accomplishments
Hospital Fund-raiser	• Helped to raise $500,000 for new hospital wing • Purchased equipment for handicapped children • Established outpatient counseling facility • Coordinated annual fashion show, netting $75,000
Assistant Food Manager for non-profit produce outlet	• Purchased foods • Determined price lists • Recruited volunteer salespeople • Kept monthly books • Wrote and distributed monthly reports to Co-op members
Administrative Assistant to State Director of Family Counseling	• Worked on brochure for annual crisis intervention lecture series • Initiated and implemented volunteer crisis alert program • Developed promotional media for child abuse prevention • Coordinated lecture series for local community groups on family counseling topics

Examples of Job Skills and Accomplishments

Job Experience (Paid or unpaid)	Accomplishments
Alumni Committee Member	• Planned and organized parent-student orientation program for incoming and transfer students • Coordinated annual phone-athon for alumni contributions • Wrote alumni news column in quarterly newsletter
Executive Secretary to President	• Edited annual company report • Supervised office of 15 staff members • Designed invitations and programs for "Meet Your Staff" luncheons • Designed and developed executive microfilm library for international conference

Now it's your turn.

Review all of the exercises you have completed in this chapter and study the examples provided. Then combine this information about yourself into a cohesive whole. Begin by listing your job experiences (as you did at the first stage). Along with these jobs, identify what you did — your achievements or accomplishments. Use action words that focus on these skills.

What you are doing is putting together a comprehensive profile of what you have to offer a potential employer. Your personality traits will also emerge. Perhaps you are a person not only with multiple skills and talents but someone who also has patience, the ability to work with people, organizational and communication skills, and persistence and reliability.

If you have been out of the job market (in order to raise a family, for example) or have spent years in a career that seems far removed from the paralegal field, then it is your challenge to convince a potential employer that you possess valuable skills that only years and varied experiences can bring: problem-solving skills and decision-making abilities, as well as diligence and determination. What employer could ask for higher qualifications?

As you review these last pages and prepare the final exercise in this chapter, you will be reviewing your past and learning how to build on your experiences.

In this final exercise, you are asked to do a summation of your work history, focusing on the skills you wish to present in your resumé. You may want to review your first job chronology draft that you completed earlier in this chapter.

Be certain to be as specific as you can in the column which asks that you include achievements or accomplishments. That information will become an important part of your resumé, the topic of the next chapter.

Work Chronology

Year	Organization	Title	Duties / Activities	Skills / Accomplishments

Skills

List the skills you have developed in your previous positions. Review what you have included on the last pages. You may also wish to review the previous chapter in which you were asked to evaluate your level of competence in various skills. Also focus on the *skill word* you will be using in your resumé.

_____

_____

_____

_____

_____

_____

_____

Qualifications

How would you summarize your qualifications? Again, review the last pages to determine what you have done in your previous jobs (paid and unpaid). Try to include your most marketable qualifications in one sentence. You will find this a helpful exercise as part of your resumé preparation.

_____

_____

_____

_____

_____

_____

_____

The Resumé

4

A resumé is a word portrait, your *professional* profile, the profile that you want to show a prospective employer. It is not a complete picture, but it does include the highlights from your background, training, and experience that you wish to emphasize. Remember, you are in control of the words on paper, and how you shape your resumé can help to focus on the areas you want recognized immediately.

Essentially, then, the resumé is your professional introduction and, while it cannot get you a job, it should help you to get an interview — and that is the purpose of the resumé.

In order to present those qualifications you wish to stress, a good resumé requires a great deal of preliminary work before you get the finished product. In the previous chapter, you were asked to do such preliminary work. Now let's see how you can put that knowledge to work.

What you may have realized by this time is that there is no one right way to write a resumé; there is no *one* format that is best for everyone. However, there is a right way and best format for you, one that will work in helping you to combine your varied background as you proceed in your job search as a paralegal.

In Chapter 3, you thoroughly examined your training, education, and experience. The importance of such an intensive self-assessment was to have you recognize what you have to offer an employer. That chapter required you to summarize what every employer is looking for in a job candidate: *your skills and accomplishments*. Keep those two words in mind. An employer wants to know why you are the best person for the job — based on what you can do (your skills) and the evidence that you have done it (your accomplishments).

How you convey those skills and accomplishments on paper may be achieved in a number of ways. Keep in mind, however, that you must clearly demonstrate that *you are the person to be called in for the interview because you are the best qualified person for the job.*

As you examine each section of the resumé, you will learn how to shape your self-assessment information to be that person.

Before beginning, however, remember that everything on your resumé must be verifiable. In a competitive job market, it might be tempting to include a degree you did not earn, a prestigious school you did not attend, a more marketable major you did not have, or a particular job title you did not hold. Who will ever know?

Aside from the ethical considerations of including erroneous or misleading information, it is far too risky to do so. If the fraud is detected, you will be eliminated from the applicant list or, if you have the job, it is most likely that you will be fired. Even an unintentional printing error of an employment data has been known to keep an otherwise attractive job candidate from being hired.

The range and reasons for such embellished data on a resumé are wide. Many actually convince themselves that they *almost* have a degree and so they include it; others believe they performed the functions of a particular position and list a job title they felt they earned. The naive assumption is that an employer will not bother to check out the information. In an attempt to appear more qualified, such a person ultimately conveys a lack of honesty and integrity.

On the other hand, it is far more likely that you will *not* give yourself credit for what you *have* achieved or for skills that you *have* developed. A closer examination of the previous chapter should help you as you prepare your resumé, whatever format you choose.

Format

The basic formats listed below are almost self-explanatory. Each has advantages and disadvantages. You can decide which is most appropriate for you once we have discussed each one and you have an opportunity to see the samples included at the end of this chapter.

The **chronological** resumé lists all education and work experience in chronology from the present to the past.

The **functional** or **skills** resumé emphasizes experiences and how they relate to the job which the candidate is seeking. This format stresses skills and achievements without focusing on the specific dates and places, although they are included.

The **combination** format blends the advantages of the chronological resumé with those of the functional resumé. It can be the most complete, the most general, as well as the most specific all at the same time. But it must be coordinated skillfully to avoid the appearance of a hodgepodge of unrelated experiences.

For the purposes of your resumé as a paralegal, it should be stressed that while you have some latitude in arranging your material and information, there are some guidelines that should prove very helpful. Let's look at each section as it should be considered.

Keep in mind an important point: most employers prefer a one-page resumé. Later on in this chapter, we discuss how you can make the best use of the margins, choice of paper, type styles, headings, and other details. You are still in a preliminary stage at this point, so it is far more essential that you get down everything you wish to include in your resumé and then see how you can combine areas or edit your information. It is far easier to edit later than to try to remember what you left out.

Resumé Categories

While the final order of your material will depend upon the format you choose and the emphasis you wish to place on certain information, it will be helpful for you to identify the major categories you want to include. Each of these points are discussed in detail in the following pages, before you put together your final resumé. Some of them are optional; others are essential.

```
Personal Information
Career Objective
Summary of Skills and Qualifications
Education
Work Experience
Professional Activities
Special Awards and Recognition
Military Experience
Special Interest/Community Activities
References
```

In order of appearance, let us now consider some essential items to be included in your resumé, regardless of the final format you choose.

Personal Information

Name   Address   Telephone

The above items are the *only* ones that you are required to provide by law. This information should be included at the top of your resumé where it will be readily seen.

Do not include the entry titles, such as *Name, Address, Area code & Telephone number* when you give this information. Do not list formal titles here or any nicknames. Such informality may demonstrate a friendliness but not professionalism.

In your address, list the place where you can be contacted when you send out your resumé. If you will have a different address after a specified date, you may list two addresses. Refer to the resumé samples for an illustration of this point.

Be sure to include a telephone number at which you are certain someone will be to answer calls. If it is an out of town number, list it, but in your cover letter explain that you will call "the recipient" at a specified time and then do so. If you cannot be available to answer your phone, ask someone to do so for you. Do not list a work phone unless you have permission to do so or know for certain that it will not prove awkward for you to receive a phone call. Today it has become generally acceptable to use an answering machine if you are not able to answer your calls personally. Keep some important points in mind, however.

- Make certain that you have left a clear, direct message with a time that you will return your calls.

- It does not seem reasonable to ask someone to call after business hours.

- Avoid cute messages designed to impress your listener. They will have the opposite effect. Remember that a potential employer may not wish to leave a message at all if *your* message is unprofessional. Do not expect a potential employer to make an unreasonable effort to contact you. There are too many other willing and available job candidates.

Other personal items which reveal your age, health, or marital status are not relevant and could possibly keep you from getting to the interview stage. You do not know what personal biases a potential employer might have. Therefore, even though you cannot be denied a job *legally* because of your age or young dependents, particularly if you are a woman, your resumé may be rejected for any number of reasons. You want to give yourself the best opportunity to get the interview. On the other hand, *do* include items that could make you more attractive for a specific job, such as willingness to relocate, if that is appropriate for you.

Career Objective

Many feel that stating a job or career objective locks them into one specific area and that they should leave all their options open by writing a general resumé. A career objective entry *is* optional, but if you decide to include it, make it work for you.

Employers are looking for people with specific skills, and a brief career objective can indicate that you are a person who has a very clear idea of where you are going.

A career objective will focus on what you think you can and would like to do, based on your skills and qualifications. It need not be lengthy, but it should add something to your resumé; otherwise, omit the category. Below are some examples which provide useful information.

- An entry-level paralegal position offering increasing responsibilities and opportunities in real estate or land development.

- To obtain a challenging paralegal position which would enable me to use my intensive generalist training and legal research skills, as well as my diverse academic and employment background.

For additional examples, study the model resumés included at the end of this section.

Again, remember that this entry is *optional.* To be vague, confusing, or redundant would be only a disadvantage for you.

Summary of Skills and Qualifications or Highlights

Although this category, Summary of Skills and Qualifications, is also optional, it can serve a useful function. It clearly focuses those skills and qualifications you have developed over the years so that an employer can readily see how they relate to a paralegal position. It can also help you pull together various types of experiences you may have developed in several different types of jobs.

In the last chapter in which you completed your self-assessment and self-inventory, you were asked to summarize the skills you had developed in your various positions, both full-time and part-time, paid and unpaid. You may wish to review that chapter and the final list in which you summarized your skills. You may want to revise the list or write a one- or two-sentence summary now.

This statement at the beginning of the resumé can help a potential employer immediately recognize what you have to offer as an employee.

The following examples may give you some idea of how to focus your own skills and qualifications in a summary statement.

Summary of Skills and Qualifications: Extensive experience in varied settings has enabled me to develop strong communication skills: specifically research, writing, and verbal and interpersonal communication. My organizational and detail-oriented background should prove to be an asset in a paralegal position.

Highlights: Strong organizational and communication skills, combined with intensive paralegal training and experience in varied legal and non-legal settings, have provided me with the necessary qualifications to perform at high-level capacity.

Review your own "highlights" and determine if they will attract the attention of an employer in a summary statement. If you decide to omit this entry, you should still review your qualifications so that you can include your most marketable qualifications in your cover letter. This point is discussed later in this chapter.

Education

It is essential for you to include this section as your first major category. An employer will want to see your education, background, and training immediately. List your education beginning with your paralegal training, where you received it, when you received it, and your specialty, if you had one. Not all programs have been approved by the American Bar Association. If your program has ABA approval, or if it is a graduate-level certificate program, be certain to include that information. You may wish to include specific courses or the hours of training, depending upon the space that you have available. Be certain, however, that you do include the significant, essential information that indicates that you are a trained paralegal. The following examples illustrate how you can list all of this information — briefly, but completely.

Review the resumé samples in the section which follows to determine how you wish to present your information. Include important details: the curriculum (your specialty or the generalist program), computer training (if relevant), and any other information you would like to emphasize, such as courses taken (if space permits). The important point is that you do not omit anything essential.

The subsequent entries under the education category should include schools you attended, dates you graduated, degrees you received, and academic majors (and minors, if applicable). Avoid listing months (and other details which will clutter your resumé). You may wish to include special academic honors you received in this section; you may also include your grade point average (G.P.A.) if it is significantly higher than a B average.

You do not need to include all of the schools you attended on a part-time or temporary basis. Use your own judgment. You may include special training or schools that provided you with relevant skills; the resumé models in this section offer some helpful guidelines. Remember to use reverse chronology in your listings; that is, give the most current information first and then work backwards.

Should you include your graduate degree or graduate study? Or will this "over-qualify" you for an entry-level position? Think of all the important skills and background you have developed. The issue is how to include this information so that it works for you.

Your job is to convince an employer that you are willing to begin at an entry-level position because you do *not* have skills and experience in this new field, but that your additional education will prove to be an asset to them and should help you to move ahead quickly. Be certain, however, that you believe this yourself before you attempt to convince anyone else.

Work Experience

This category may just as easily be entitled: Work History, Employment Record, Professional Experience, or any other title which is descriptive of the employment information you are about to list.

In this section it is important for you to tell where you worked, the dates (years), your title, and what you did on the job. *Do not omit dates.* Employers will want to verify where you worked and when. It's also essential for you to proofread your final resumé carefully for the accuracy of dates. A typographical error has actually cost some applicants the job! Do not distinguish part-time from full-time jobs, paid from volunteer work. You may wish to group summer jobs you held to finance your education. The completed resumés at the end of this chapter illustrate the widely varied ways in which you can include this information.

Most of the preparation for this category has already been completed in the previous chapter. Review that section, particularly the part in which you were asked to identify your skills by using action verbs.

Include all of your jobs and indicate what skills you developed, skills that could prove to be an asset to an organization. If you have not had extensive job experience, you may include skills developed in your college activities or in volunteer work. Internships may be included in this section if your work experience is limited. Otherwise, you may include any internships under the education category.

Be careful of the accuracy of your dates in your work history; this information will very likely be verified by someone interested in hiring you.

If you wish to de-emphasize the exact chronology of years, particularly if you have been out of the job market for some years, you may wish to use a functional format, one in which skills are emphasized in clusters and the chronology of events is listed at the end of the resumé. Examine the model resumés if you think such a format is appropriate for you.

Other categories on your resumé may be optional. If you have special honors or awards, include them so an employer can identify you as someone with unique talents and achievements. If you have been involved in community activities, a category may be included to indicate the level of responsibilities and skills you have developed.

If you have military service, include it as a separate category.

If you have special skills and training, such as foreign language proficiency or computer or other technical skills, include them.

Remember that your resumé is your professional profile, so think of the person who will be reading it. Does yours reflect what you have done and what you are capable of doing? Have you focused on your skills and accomplishments? That is what an employer will be looking for.

As your final entry, simply list the statement: References available upon request.

It is not appropriate to include a list of your references. You may be asked to include them on a job application, or in your cover letter you may include someone in the organization who knows you and has referred you to this position. You may also wish to take a list of your references to the job interview and leave them with the interviewer, if it seems appropriate for you to do so. And remember: ALWAYS ask your references for permission to use their names and indicate that they may be contacted.

Finally, take time to study the resumé models which follow the summary guidelines for developing an effective resumé.

Guidelines for Developing an Effective Resumé

Appearance

1. Choose high-quality paper (twenty-five pound rag content), either white bond, off-white, gray, or beige. The latter colors will offer distinction without distraction. However, you should use matching color envelopes if you use these shades.

2. With so many professional processes available today, it will not be difficult for you to choose one that will make your resumé take on the professional appearance you want. Many print shops will photocopy your resumé inexpensively. If you choose this process, be certain that *yours* is flawless and that the typing looks professional and is completely camera ready. You may wish to have your resumé typeset and find that the price difference is so small that it will be worth the investment. Today, laser printing is equally acceptable. This process is available if you have access to a computer. The final product has a professional appearance, but you must carefully proofread your copy. Dot-matrix copies are *not* suitable for final resumés.

Never use carbons or poorly reproduced typed copies of your resumé. It also goes without saying that handwritten resumés are never acceptable, no matter how fine or elegant your handwriting.

3. Standard paper size is 8½ inches by 11 inches. You should keep to standard size; your envelope may be regulation business size or you may use the larger size to match your resumé.

4. Typing should be error free. An electric or electronic typewriter will provide clean copy for the printer. If you are having your resumé typeset or are using a computer with a laser printer, you might consider use of different sized lettering, bold face, and italics for emphasis. Remember that no matter how you have your resumé duplicated, *you* are ultimately responsible for any misspellings, typographical errors or printer's errors. Be certain to proofread your final copy before leaving your typist or printer.

5. Use capital letters sparingly. The same hold true for underlining. The purpose of these devices is to make an item stand out. If they are overused, nothing will stand out. Some of the sample resumés included in this book will demonstrate the effective use of both.

6. Do not abbreviate. All organizations' names (for example, American Medical Association, American Management Association) should be spelled out. Degrees, special awards, and all titles should also be spelled out fully.

7. If the institutional or organizational name of a former employer has been changed, indicate the current name as well as the former name. For example: Carnegie-Mellon University, formerly Carnegie Institute of Technology, or AMGRO, formerly American Textile Growth Corporation.

8. Be consistent in your layout and composition. Complete sentences will take up valuable space, but be certain that your phrases are grammatically correct and free from ambiguity.

9. Use past tense for previous activities, experiences, or acquired skills. Present tense refers to ongoing or current activities.

10. Consult a dictionary for correct spellings. If you are a poor speller, have someone else proofread your final copy. It is also a good idea to have someone else proofread your final copy from the printer, if at all possible.

11. Use white space for eye appeal and easy reading. Use ample margins and make certain they are uniform. Use indentions and tabs for best use of white space and emphasis of key points. If you have extensive information you want to include on your resumé, you may be tempted to cram in as much as possible to fit it onto one page. Doing so will use up the margins,

as well as make it difficult to read. You want an employer to be able to easily identify the skills and experiences that you have. One solution to this problem is to have your resumé typeset so that you can take advantage of smaller size print in some categories.

12. Edit your resumé so that you include all the essential points, but avoid unnecessary details. Do not ramble on, nor include a philosophical statement about yourself, your profession, or the world in general. If an employer wants to get to know you, you will be called in for an interview.

13. Watch your language. Avoid jargon. Do not use pompous or self-serving descriptions, such as *invaluable, highly creative, sensitive,* or *perceptive.* Let your reader judge on the basis of what your credentials and accomplishments say about you.

14. Constantly update your resumé. Never send an old resumé to which you have added recent items. If an important event, such as the receipt of an honor or award, occurs after your current resumé has been printed, you may include the specific item in your cover letter.

15. Your resumé will be a reflection of you — your style, as well as your history of professional accomplishments. Therefore, you should not allow anyone else to write it for you. Suggestions and comments from others are helpful insofar as they can improve what you say or what you omit. But your style and format should be as unique and individual as you are.

Sample Career Objectives

- Experienced paralegal seeks position using background in library science and legal research.

- A challenging paralegal position involving coordinating, communicating, and researching, with opportunity for growth.

- An entry-level paralegal position to use my experience in real estate sales and marketing, in combination with my training in legal research specializing in real estate.

Sample Highlights

- Professional paralegal with corporate experience in Patents and Trademarks, Anti-Trust Litigation, Bankruptcy, and Legal Research. Supervisory and administrative background, coupled with strong verbal and written communication skills.

- Professional paralegal specializing in corporate real estate acquisitions with proven results in developing innovative cost-savings procedures.

- Extensive experience in legal environments have enabled me to develop strong communication skills: specifically, research and writing. Additional intensive training in a generalist curriculum has broadened the scope and depth of my understanding of the duties and responsibilities of a paralegal.

Sample Employment Descriptions

- Researched, compiled, and wrote corporate report documents.

- Developed methods and procedures to ensure efficient work flow.

- Supervised hiring and management of clerical and paralegal employees.

- Analyzed and reviewed preparation of tariff filings for submission to the Civil Aeronautics Board.

Sample Community/Professional Activities

- Guest Lecturer: Illinois Paralegal Association.

- Designed and presented salary negotiation seminar.

- Campaign Coordinator: Managed all aspects of local drug awareness program for elementary and junior high school students, including press releases, contacting speakers, and moderating panel.

Sample Resumés

The following pages provide sample resumés. They illustrate different formats and techniques that have been discussed in this chapter. As you review these, note the differences in the chronological versus the functional or skills resumés.

Mary Sue O'Brien
360 Greenleaf Road
Northfield, Illinois 60048
Day: (708) 328-1234   Evening: (708) 541-5678

OBJECTIVE: A paralegal/administrative assistant position utilizing my estates, trusts and wills background and client relations skills.

EDUCATION:
1991 **ROOSEVELT UNIVERSITY**, Chicago, Illinois.
Lawyer's Assistant Program
ABA approved, graduate-level certificate.
Estates, Trusts and Wills specialty. Curriculum included:
- Probate, estate, and gift taxes, and estate planning (including minimizing income and death taxes and achieving estate objectives)
- Legal research and writing
- Computer applications with IBM PC (Lotus 1-2-3, dBASE III)

1989 **UNIVERSITY OF ILLINOIS**, Urbana/Champaign.
Bachelor of Science
Psychology major, Business minor (Grade point average 4.3/5.0)

EXPERIENCE:
1987 - present **LEGAL ASSISTANT/SECRETARY**
John A. Looby, Attorney at Law, Evanston, Illinois.
Draft and prepare wills, trusts, probate documents, individual, fiduciary, and estate tax returns and real estate closing documents. Telephone and written correspondence, bookkeeping, billing, payroll, and office reception.

1986-87 **CUSTOMER SERVICE REPRESENTATIVE**
(seasonal) *Ravinia Festival Association, Highland Park, Illinois.*
Answered inquiries, accepted ticket orders and resolved complaints of contributors, performers, and general public. Assisted with general office and accounting duties and implemented sales projects for management.

1987 **RESEARCH ASSISTANT**
Psychology Department, University of Illinois, Champaign.
Researched interpersonal conflict resolution procedures. Interviewed and observed subjects, operated experiment equipment, and assisted with computer coding and statistical analysis of data.

HONORS: Psi Chi National Honor Society in Psychology
Dean's List 1986, 1987 and 1988.

REFERENCES: Furnished upon request.

Carl Anderson
6345 College Oak Drive
Sacramento, CA 95481
(714) 662-5555

Education

California College of Paralegal Studies
Sherman Oaks, California, 1991
Certificate Program for the Legal Assistant
Certificate of Completion - Corporations

University of California, Berkeley, California, 1991
Bachelor of Arts
Major: Political Science
Dean's List: Four semesters (Grade point average 3.93)

WBBM TV, Los Angeles, California, 1990
Internship: Newswriting and Production

West Coast Today, Redwood City, California, 1989
Internship: Newsgathering and Reporting
Redwood City Council

Employment History

The Banker's Life, Fresno, California, 1991
Special Agent. Designed and marketed insurance-related aspects of employee benefit plans.

The Metropolitan Life, Hayward, California, 1990
Sales Representative. Prepared and marketed multi-line insurance and financial programs to individual and small groups.

Navistar (International Harvester Company),
Hayward, California, 1989-1990
Quality Analyst. Managed material inventory and distribution. Performed wide range of operations in product quality and planning.

Military Service

United States Army, 1985-1989
Communications Specialist: AFVN Radio and Television, Saigon.
Wrote, produced, and reported news, music, and promotional segments. Awarded Army Commendation Medal. Honorable discharge.

Community Affairs

President, Blackhawk Forest Homeowner's Association. Organized 5,000 homeowners to pursue and gain passage of water quality legislation through California General Assembly.

References and writing samples available upon request.

Helen Adams
2674 Bay Area Boulevard
Houston, Texas 60187
(713) 964-5588

EDUCATION

1989	University of Houston at Clear Lake City, Houston, Texas Legal Studies Program Real Estate

1988	University of Houston at Clear Lake City, Houston, Texas Bachelor of Arts Major: Psychology Minor: Communication

INTERNSHIP

1987	Texas Institute of Development Disabilities Assisted developmentally disabled and mentally retarded teenagers and children in hospital setting.

WORK EXPERIENCE

1988-1991	Top Realty, Houston, Texas Office Manager Researched and selected prospective customers for potential sale of property; served as liaison to customer and agent; handled customer service replies; sold home, health, and life insurance; managed day-to-day office operations.

1982-1987	Financed 50% of college education with various part-time positions such as cashier, receptionist, bookkeeper, ad counselor, and clerk. Recipient of Illinois State Scholarship for four years.

SKILLS AND INTERESTS

Photographer, Church Council News
Computer programming experience in
FORTRAN and COBOL

References available upon request.

Allison Parker
7000 Roswell Road NE
Atlanta, Georgia 30328
(404) 742-8812

OBJECTIVE: A responsible paralegal position which will enable me to use my professional training, business background, and language skills.

EDUCATION

1991   The National Center for Paralegal Training
Atlanta, Georgia
Generalist Program

Intensive training in civil and criminal litigation, real estate, corporations, estates, trusts and wills, debtor-creditor relationships, family law, legal research, and computer literacy.

1985   Florida State University, Tallahassee
Bachelor of Arts, cum laude
Major: Business   Minors: Psychology, Spanish

EMPLOYMENT

1988-1990   Voyager Financial Services, Jacksonville, Florida
Brokerage Technician for insurance company's leading brokers. Processed insurance and investment product applications. Provided services for existing accounts.

1984-1986   Broward & Barnett, Jacksonville, Florida
Sale Manager. Supervised sales agents, estate and tax planning specialists in manufacture of financial planning reports for clients. Analyzed clients' assets, prepared materials for computer illustrations and word processing and management reports.

COMMUNITY ACTIVITIES

Project leader, Adult Literacy Program in the Hispanic community. Sigma Lambda Chi Honors Fraternity, Scholarship Chairperson. Organist, Community Bible Church, Jacksonville.

References available upon request.

Ruth Martin
176 South Street
Garden City, New York 11530
(516) 667-3729

CAREER OBJECTIVE: To find a challenging paralegal position that would enable me to use my intensive generalist paralegal training, diverse academic and employment background.

EDUCATION

1991   Adelphi University, Huntington, New York
Lawyer's Assistant Program
Generalist Curriculum
ABA Approved, Graduate Level Certificate Program

1988   Syracuse University, Syracuse, New York
Bachelor of Science in Education

Junior academic year: Switzerland
Special studies in educational theory and practice.

EMPLOYMENT

1988-1991   Member, Planning Team for Curriculum Reorganization
Conducted research for educational planning, implemented and evaluated pilot programs for six-school system. Wrote daily reports. Directed student teachers, served as master teacher in all subjects of program.

Board of Education of New York City, Brooklyn, New York

1984-1988   Various positions held to finance 80% of college education.

1986-1988   Proof Operator. Marine Midland Bank, Syracuse, New York
Encoded checks for all Workman's Compensation Fund accounts. Developed debit/credit accuracy check system. Trained new operators to work on specialized projects with time deadlines.

1984-1987   File Clerk. Cortland Memorial Hospital, Syracuse, New York
Reorganized and maintained comprehensive filing system of hospital outpatient records. Developed medical terminology reference guide.

1982-1985   Library Assistant. Syracuse University Library, Syracuse, New York
Worked with collection and acquisition librarian.
Processed and maintained periodical files.

INTERESTS   Outdoor photography. Member, Conservationists Club.
Volunteer, Teenage Alcohol Rehabilitation Center.

References Available Upon Request.

Anne M. Smith
1021 Wood Hollow Drive
Marietta, Georgia 30067
(404) 358-7767

Summary of Skills and Qualifications:

Extensive experience in varied settings has enabled me to develop strong communication skills: specifically, research, writing, and verbal and interpersonal skills. My organizational and detail-oriented background should prove to be an asset in a paralegal position.

EDUCATION

1991   Lawyer's Assistant Program of The National Center for Paralegal Training, Atlanta, Georgia.
Specialty in Corporations with training in Legal Research, General Practice, and Computer Literacy.

1987   University of Georgia, Athens, Georgia.
Bachelor of Arts, Cum Laude
Major: English   Minors: Sociology, Psychology

PROFESSIONAL SKILLS

Communication

- Completed individual and background checks
- Developed and wrote reports based on research
- Researched and planned audio-visual presentations
- Worked with clients in sales capacity

Management/Supervisory

- Managed financial affairs of condominium co-op
- Handled purchase orders for retail merchandise
- Supervised sales department of major retail firm
- Screened and interviewed new management trainees

Organizational

- Collaborated on development and implementation of multi-disciplinary study program
- Participated in restructuring of departmental policies regarding outside funding
- Member, President's Commission on Fiscal Priorities

WORK EXPERIENCE

1989-1991   Equifax Services, Atlanta, Georgia. Field Investigator.
1987-1989   Fermi Lab, Batavia, Illinois. Team Analyst, Government Services.
1985-1987   Webster's Department Store, Athens, Georgia. Retail sales and inventory.

References available upon request.

Michael Johnson
1822 N. Walnut Street
Flushing, NY 11366
(212) 442-5699

EDUCATION

Certificate, Lawyer's Assistant Program
Corporations Specialty
Adelphi University, Huntington, New York, 1991
- ABA Approved
- Graduate Level
- Legal Research Training

Bachelor of Science, Purdue University,
West Lafayette, Indiana, 1987
Major: Civil Engineering

SKILLS

COMMUNICATION

- Edited technical papers for publication
- Prepared monthly current literature column
- Compiled index for monthly periodical
- Conducted interviews for staff personnel

TECHNICAL

- Researched and developed plant operating manuals
- Used research aids and wrote legal memoranda
- Investigated and analyzed engineering problems

ORGANIZATIONAL

- Coordinated design, construction of new facilities
- Established daily operating procedures for 4 plants
- Supervised 25 operators and mechanics

WORK EXPERIENCE

- Assistant Editor, Air Pollution Control Association Pittsburgh, Pennsylvania, 1989-1990
- Engineer, Power & Fuels Dept., Inland Steel Company, East Chicago, Indiana, 1987-1989
- Staff Writer, *Exponent*, Purdue University West Lafayette, Indiana, 1985-1987

REFERENCES

Available upon request.

SUSAN G. STONE

718 Franklin Road
Huntington, West Virginia 23219
(804) 863-5566

(After December 15, 1991)
P.O. Box 1041
Miami, Florida 33161
(305) 267-4324

EDUCATION

1991   **Pensacola Junior College**, Pensacola, Florida.
Concentration in Civil and Criminal Litigation with training in
Corporate Law, Real Estate, and Probate.

1986   **Marshall University**, Huntington, West Virginia.
Bachelor of Arts in Education.

EXPERIENCE

**Administrative/
Management**
Organized student government programs and activities
Managed student governmental fund-raising and
     supervised disbursements
Coordinated teachers' efforts to implement mathematics
     pilot program
Maintained inventory system for juvenile and social
     science books
Assisted customers with problems and requests

Communication
Completed classroom assignments in legal writing,
     including briefing cases, drafting legal
     documents, and writing memos
Researched, wrote, and implemented many
     instructional units for various grade levels
Designed and completed a quarter-long independent
     study project
Developed interpersonal skills through retail sales

Teaching
Instructed adults in workshops and in-service training
     involving mathematics pilot program and
     school-based instructional improvement
Taught 7th and 8th graders in student government
     and 2nd through 4th graders in mixed-
     grade classrooms

Employment

1990-91
B. Dalton Bookstore, Pineville, West Virginia,
     retail sales.

1984-89
Woodrow Wilson Elementary School, Sanford,
     West Virginia, teacher

References   Furnished upon request

Paul Jones
2020 North Harding Avenue
Chicago, Illinois 60623
(312) 927-7531

**PROFESSIONAL
OBJECTIVE**

A challenging position in a legal environment which will enable me to use my extensive verbal, interpersonal, and research communication skills as a paralegal.

EDUCATION
1991

Roosevelt University, Chicago, Illinois
Lawyer's Assistant Program: Certificate
Graduate Level ABA Approved Curriculum
Litigation, Legal Research, and Computer Literacy

1986

Art Institute of Chicago/Goodman Theater
Bachelor of Fine Arts in Technical Direction

EXPERIENCE

Communication
- University Instructor in Technical Direction
- Worked closely with personnel from varied socio-economic and educational backgrounds
- Created and implemented computer system for internal control of merchandise flow

Management/Supervision
- Supervised and coordinated 10-150 person crew
- Directed and executed cost estimating and purchasing of tools, equipment, materials
- Supervised year-round operation of all studios

Design
- Designed and renovated three-story building for film and television studio
- Designed over 195 theatrical productions

Technical
- Operations Coordinator/Designer
- Technical Director/Set and Lighting Designer
- Film/Special Effects Director
- Proficient in reading, drafting and designing blueprints

EMPLOYMENT
1984-1990
1980-1984
1976-1980
1974-1976

Operations Designer, William Harrison Studios
Foreman, Stage Manager, Northwestern University
Technical Director/Designer, Florida State University
Associate Instructor, Indiana University Theater

REFERENCES

Available upon request.

Margaret Garland
294 Green Street
Madison, New Jersey 07940
(201) 980-4879

PROFESSIONAL OBJECTIVE

A challenging position in an environment which will enable me to use my interpersonal skills and paralegal training.

EDUCATION

1991   Fairleigh Dickinson University, Madison, New Jersey. Paralegal Studies Program Certificate. General Practice Curriculum: Corporations, Litigation, Real Estate and Mortgages, Estates, Trusts and Wills, Criminal Law, and Legal Research.

1991   St. John's University, Jamaica, New York.
Bachelor of Science: Major -   Social Work
                                 Minor -   Criminal Justice

EXPERIENCE

COMMUNICATION SKILLS
- Worked with clientele from diverse backgrounds
- Provided customer assistance and information
- Contacted suppliers by telephone and letter

NEGOTIATION SKILLS
- Arranged for and executed purchasing of materials
- Coordinated deliveries

ORGANIZATIONAL SKILLS
- Assisted in planning presentation of stock
- Assisted in compiling inventory reports
- Implemented filing system to follow up orders

EMPLOYMENT

1982-Present   Child care and homemaker

1985-1987   Cashier/Baker, Parker Foods, Valley Stream, New York

1980-1982   Traffic Engineer Assistant, Village of Morton Park, New York

1978-1980   Social Work Intern, Herrick House, Queens, New York

REFERENCES   Available upon request

Final Checklist for Resumé Categories/ Information

Name
Address
Phone
Career Objective
Highlights or Summary of Skills and Qualifications
Education:
- Schools
- Years
- Certificates
- Degrees
- Major Course of Study
- Specialized Training
- Honors (G.P.A. if appropriate)
- Internships
- Special Activities/Projects

Employment:
- Years
- Job Title
- Employer and Locale
- Job Responsibilities/Skills Developed
- Major Accomplishments
- Promotions

Professional Activities:
- Years
- Active Memberships/Title of Organizations
- Offices Held/Involvements
- Major Accomplishments

Community (Volunteer) Activities:
- Years
- Titles of Organizations/Programs
- Specific Participation (Involvement, Offices Held)
- Major Accomplishments

Special Skills: Foreign Languages, Technical Skills, etc.
Military Service
Interests
References: Available upon request.

The Cover Letter

5

Whether you are applying for a job that is listed in the want ads or any other place, your best chance for recognition will be the result of a clear, direct cover letter attached to your resumé. A good cover letter is well focused and specifically tailored to the job for which you are applying. While you probably have a standard resumé that you will include for all job applications, *every* cover letter should be individual. To make this task easier, there are basic guidelines that apply to all the cover letters you write.

1. If possible, find out the name of the person who is handling the interviews for the job.

2. If the company is listed in the phone book, you usually can call and request the information.

3. What if only a box number is listed? There are varying views on how to address such a letter. All of them leave a great deal to be desired.

   "Dear Box 203A," "To Whom It May Concern," "Gentlemen," and "Madam" are considered to be the least preferable. "Dear Sir" has fallen into the sexist language category, and it might work against you — particularly if the interviewer happens to be a woman.

   "Dear Personnel Manager" could be used if you wish to be conservative and still remain professional.

4. Let good taste always be your guide but, if at all possible, find out the name of the person who will be reading your letter.

5. Demonstrate that you understand the requirements of the position and that you have the credentials and qualifications to fulfill those requirements.

6. Include examples of specific results you have obtained that are relevant to the job.

7. Focus on key points of your resumé that emphasize your capabilities and experience.

8. Avoid any negative or apologetic remarks concerning qualifications you do *not* have for the job.

9. Be confident and positive about the qualities you do have, without sounding arrogant.

10. Emphasize how you can meet any important need of the company.

11. Do not ramble or include any personal philosophical statements. Your letter should stand independent of your resumé — it must be to the point and directly related to the job.

12. Keep your letter to one page. You will have time to expand your remarks and impress your interviewer in person. If that person is bored by a too-long letter, you may never get to that stage.

13. Proofread the typed letter carefully. Typographical errors or misspellings will reflect negatively on you and may cost you an interview.

The order of your remarks should be straightforward. The following formula may be a helpful guide.

1. *Opening: Capture your reader's interest.* Indicate where and how you found out about the job. If it was a newspaper ad, include the name of the paper and the date. If a mutual acquaintance referred you, be sure to include the name of the person. Also include a sentence or two about how and why you feel you could be an asset to the company.

2. *Middle: Create a desire to meet you.* You can do this by demonstrating how specific achievements or results make you uniquely qualified for the job. You may do this by referring to some part of your resumé or by alluding to a particular award or recognition you have received in the field. You may also stress how a particular experience has provided you with useful insights into the field or job. It is also appropriate to refer specifically to the company's goals and objectives and how you could help meet them if you are hired. This section is particularly important for those who feel that they do not have the specific (or preferred) qualifications stated in the ad, but can bring other positive qualities to the job. It is also an opportunity for those who have been out of the job market for some time or who are changing careers to emphasize what they can bring to the job from their own background and professional experiences. Remember, volunteer work should not be distinguished from paid employment. Your skills and achievements should be the focal point.

3. *Ending: Stimulate action.* Request a personal interview, but leave the door open for you to make the call for an appointment, rather than waiting to hear from them. For example, you can end your letter by saying, "I look

forward to discussing this position with you further and will call your office in a few days to request an appointment."

You will, of course, want to add your own individual style to your letter, but some of the guidelines given above should help you set the tone of your letter and give you a direction to follow.

The cover letter often can be the deciding point on who is selected for the interview. And like any other part of your job search strategy, how well you are prepared in getting the job is every bit as important as how well you are prepared for the job.

Now examine the sample cover letters included. Notice how they have enabled the various applicants to tailor their specific qualifications to a job. Also notice the skill involved in pulling out those achievements and credentials directly related to the job..

Think about your own specific assets and how you can best relate them in your own cover letters. Doing so can help you convince a potential employer that you could very well be the best person for the job.

Following are 10 steps to writing a persuasive cover letter.

10 Steps to Writing a Persuasive Cover Letter

1. Discover your unique strengths that could prove to be an asset to this particular employer.

2. Focus on the specific achievements or skills you have developed in a recent job or situation (you may find these on your resumé) and highlight them in your letter.

3. Emphasize the positive qualities and relevant experiences you bring to this job — *not* what you don't have.

4. Read the job ad *very carefully*. What are they looking for? In specific language? How do they list the requirements, preferred or essential? What is their wording? Tailor your qualifications to their needs. If they are looking for someone with specific skills, be certain to mention, in the exact same language, what you have to offer them. Doing so will let them see how exactly right you are for the job!

5. Do not cross the line from being confident to being overbearing. Let the tone of your letter indicate that both you and the company would mutually benefit from what you have to offer, not that this is a great career step for you.

6. Avoid any rambling statements about the field or why you entered it: you may have an opportunity to talk about this in an interview. On the other

hand, you may emphasize that the job offers you an opportunity to build on skills and achievements from the past, even in a different field.

7. Close your letter with an action statement: how do you plan to follow up? Let your reader know when you plan to call and then follow through on your plan.

8. Proofread your letters carefully and be certain to have the correct spelling of names, as well as the proper titles and degrees, if appropriate.

9. Keep your letter to one page, with well-spaced paragraphs for easier reading.

10. Choose high-quality paper to reflect a polished, professional image. Remember: this letter is your introduction on paper.

On the following pages are four sample cover letters.

2345 N. Lake Street
Chicago, IL 60601
October 11, 1991

Ms. Marierose Alcocer
Midwest Realty Corporation
1822 W. Madison
Chicago, IL 60607

Ms. Alcocer:

Gary Adelman of your Finance Department has informed me of a
paralegal opening in your corporation. He feels that my background and
training qualify me for this position and has suggested that I apply.

As a recent graduate of Roosevelt University's Lawyer's Assistant
Program with a specialty in Real Estate and Mortgages, I have strongly
developed skills in this particular area. In addition, I have had practical
experience in working with a small realty firm, performing a wide variety
of duties. Such training and experience could make me an asset to your firm.

I will call your office within the next week to set up an appointment to
discuss this position.

Thank you for your interest and consideration, and I look forward to
meeting you.

Sincerely yours,

Jean Pevan

4242 W. State Street
New York, NY 10047
April 7, 1991

Mr. Michael Hiton
Cooley, Carson & Hall
The World Trade Center
New York, NY 10047

Dear Mr. Hiton:

As one of the city's largest law firms specializing in litigation, Cooley, Carson & Hall can assuredly use the services of a paralegal with an excellent academic record and strong communication skills.

Recently, I received my certificate from the Lawyer's Assistant Program of Adelphi University with a specialty in Litigation. In addition to this intensive training, I feel that my undergraduate studies in political science and English have prepared me for a successful career as a paralegal.

I would like to discuss the possibilities of an entry-level position with your firm and will call your office within the next week to set up an appointment.

Thank you for your interest and consideration, and I look forward to meeting you.

Sincerely yours,

Gordon Shore

320 Roswell Rd NE
Atlanta, GA 30067
September 24, 1991

Mr. Todd Beauchamp
Adams, Carnes & Winters
1700 Peachtree Road NE
Atlanta, GA 30326

Dear Mr. Beauchamp:

In response to your ad in the *Atlanta Constitution* of September 22, I would like to apply for the paralegal position listed by your firm.

Recently, I graduated with honors from The National Center for Paralegal Training. In addition to the intensive paralegal courses, I received computer training and developed strong research skills.

My experience as a legal clerk over the last three years has also given me the opportunity to become familiar with legal procedures. Combined with my undergraduate studies in public administration, this experience and training should contribute to my effectiveness as a future paralegal.

I would like to discuss employment opportunities at Adams, Carnes & Winters and how my skills and qualifications can meet your needs.

Thank you for your interest and consideration. I will call your office within the next week to set up an appointment at some time convenient to you.

Sincerely yours,

Sheri L. McCoy

2800 W. Oak Street
Jacksonville, FL 32256
April 21, 1991

Ms. Pamela Thomas
First Reserve Bank of Madison
654 Grace Street
Richmond, VA 23219

Dear Ms. Thomas:

As a recent graduate of the American Institute for Paralegal Studies, I am interested in finding a position which would enable me to utilize my skills and experience.

In addition to my paralegal training at the American Institute, I feel that I can bring additional qualities to this position. While teaching in the Jacksonville Public School System, I developed a community program which enabled gifted students to work in local organizations and companies. One such project specifically focused on the banking industry. For three years I worked closely with all levels of banking personnel so that I could determine their needs and analyze how young people could make a contribution to this important aspect of our economy. In doing so, I recognized that my educational background in accounting and additional paralegal training would uniquely qualify me to perform paralegal functions within this setting.

At this time, I would like to meet with you about possible paralegal positions at First Reserve Bank and discuss how the qualifications I have described could make me an asset to your organization.

I will call your office in the next few days to set up an appointment.

Thank you for your interest and consideration.

Sincerely yours,

Steve Goranson

How to Get Hired: The Art of Being Interviewed

6

The word "interview" stems from the French word *entre-voir*, "to see each other." If we take that meaning one step further, we see in a current English dictionary that the word "interview" literally means "to see each other *mutually*." In other words, the scope and purpose of the interview is to find out if the job candidate and potential employer are "right" for each other. On both sides, it's a risk. So, basically, the interviewing process enables both parties to find out about each other, to "see" each other. It's important to understand this basic point because it emphasizes how and why an applicant should prepare thoroughly for this final step of the job search.

Of all the preceding stages, the interview is the single most important step: it's the final selling job you must do. And you must learn to do it well. Part of the problem, however, is that many people feel that they have no idea of what they will be asked and so they don't feel they can prepare for it.

This chapter not only dispels that myth; it shows you the steps to take in preparation for a successful interview.

First of all, it is important to recognize that the interview is an anxiety-producing, stress-filled situation. Of course it is. You have put in long hours, hard work, and a great deal of money preparing for the big job interview. And who likes to be rejected?

You must also remember that the interview is often an irrational, subjective process. A partial reason for this is that people don't realize that although they look competent and qualified on paper (the resumé, the cover letter), in person they come across in quite a different way. After all, it's the *person* who gets hired. And that is what this chapter is all about: showing you how to present yourself, "sell" yourself, if you will, as the best person for the job.

That leads us to the basic negotiation going on in the interview. The question is, from the interviewer, "Why should I hire *you*?" And the answer from the interviewee must be: "Because I am the best person for the job."

If you keep the basic question in mind, then all of your answers to questions during the interview will be geared to support your contention that you are the best person for the job.

Keeping that basic point in mind, let's now examine the steps you can take in developing successful interviewing strategies.

Let's reiterate a basic point. For most people, a great part of the fear of being interviewed comes from the fear of the unknown — what is going to happen? And the key to success in interviewing for jobs is the same key you have used for every previous part of your job campaign: *preparation.*

You may think that an interview may last only thirty minutes to an hour, and so much preparation time could not possibly be warranted. After all, don't they know everything about you? Not quite. They do not know you. Those interview minutes will be the most important time in your entire job campaign.

Your interview preparation should consist of what you need to find out about the organization, the job you are applying for, and if possible, the person who will be interviewing you.

Interview Preparation

Information On the Organization

Gain as much information as you can on the company or firm. Who are the key executives? How large is the organization? Number of employees? Volume of sales? Are they a product organization? Service organization? Do they hire paralegals? If so, how many? And for how long have they been there?

The more you know about the company, the better prepared you will be to see how *you* fit in. You will also save valuable time during the interview. If you have taken the time and the effort to do your homework, you will impress your interviewer as someone who is truly interested in the job.

Where will you find this information? If it's a large or established firm, either there will be reports or the information will be included in one of the publications listed in the Appendix of this book.

Also, remember your personal contacts. Do you know anyone who works for the organization or who knows someone who does? Professional associations are also a good source of information on companies.

Information On the Job for Which You Are Applying

Find out as much as you can about paralegal positions within the organization, using the same resources mentioned above. In addition, the more you can discuss your role as a paralegal and how you can be an asset to the company, the more you will impress your interviewer.

It is also perfectly acceptable for *you* to have questions about the job and the role of the paralegal within the organization. Intelligent and thoughtful questions will also demonstrate your professional interest in the field, as well as the position.

Information On the Interviewer

Find out the exact name of the interviewer, if at all possible, either over the phone when the interview is scheduled or from the receptionist when you come in to the interview. Make certain that you have the correct name and correct pronunciation. There are instances in which interviewers who have been otherwise impressed by a candidate have ruled out that person because that person made an error in pronouncing the interviewer's name.

Any other relevant information about the interviewer may prove very useful to you, if it is available: what the interviewer does within the company, the interviewer's background, etc. The purpose of such information is not to make you offer contrived statements, but rather, to illustrate that you are sufficiently interested in the position to find out as much about the company and its staff as you can. Such knowledge or information will come out in subtle ways, of course. On the other hand, it will confirm in the interviewer's mind that you are a person with similar interests, one who is compatible — if you do share these interests. In other words, you are getting the interviewer to see you as a person and to like you.

Two final suggestions: students should not hesitate to ask their teachers and/ or the paralegal program staff if they know anything about a firm. Also, when you are called for an interview with a firm that you have not heard of, ask a few questions: What kind of law does this firm practice? How large is it? You needn't spend an extraordinary amount of time over the phone asking questions before you interview, but a few basic questions reveal your interest in the firm *and* will give you some idea of the kind of work paralegals do on the job.

In preparing yourself for the interview, try to put yourself in the place of the person who will be interviewing you.

Preparing Yourself for the Interview

He or she is interested in finding an employee who can make a contribution to the company, get along with other employees, and promote the image that the company wants to project. In other words, your *professional appearance* and *behavior* may single you out and rate you higher than other applicants whose credentials may be as good as yours or even better.

Remember that your qualifications have already been submitted and have been recognized as outstanding. The purpose of the interview is for a potential employer to assess you: to measure your professional attitude about your work, to evaluate your experience and accomplishments as they relate to this particular job, and to determine how effectively you handle yourself in a stressful situation — your interpersonal and verbal communications skills. If these were not essential characteristics to an employer, the resumé itself would have gotten you the job!

What Are the Employers Looking For?

According to a recent survey, employers want a person with strong organizational skills, competence, reliability, flexibility, and the ability to become a part of the team. They want to know how you will fit in.

The fact of the matter is that personal chemistry often sells a candidate. You would do well to focus on some of the following intangible areas in order to make that important first impression as positive as possible.

It is impossible to change your personality radically, nor would you want to. You might consider, however, ways in which you can tailor your image to suit a company's needs. If you feel that your individuality is being threatened by conforming to a dress code of a company, for example, remember that the choice is yours in whether or not to apply for a position within a particular company. Generally speaking, certain traits are desirable in a job applicant. They are part of the packaging that will enable the interviewer to size you up in the first minute or two — the time in which it takes us to form our first impressions (impressions which, incidentally, are very hard to overcome — think of your own personal experiences with negative impressions you have formed of certain people, impressions which later proved to be erroneous). This important first impression, therefore, influences all the subsequent impressions — and frequently determines whether or not you are offered the job. What goes into creating this favorable first impression and how can you work on creating the impression you want to convey?

First of all, let's eliminate the notion that this discussion is about superficialities or mere externals. That is often the argument for those who disagree with the "first impression" theory. We are talking about presenting a professional package that gives an interviewer an immediate idea of who you are, based on what he or she sees. The interview itself will either support or invalidate this first impression, but why take the chance on having an impression work against you?

The first clue to your professionalism is your personal grooming. Your employer will try to see you in the job. What should you wear? When in doubt, err on the side of being conservative. High quality clothes rather than trendy outfits are a good investment. Your wardrobe should not distract from you in any way. If you are apprehensive about the appropriateness of your outfit, you can always follow the example of one woman who stood outside an office and waited until the employees came out for lunch so that she could see what *they* were wearing.

Good grooming entails more than your clothes, however. Shined shoes, manicured nails, and appropriately styled hair are essential. Heavy make-up, heady perfume, chewing gum, sunglasses, dangling jewelry, shirts without jackets or ties — all can build up a negative impression.

Following is a list of major personal and professional traits which interviewers have identified as positive qualities:

- Professional appearance and behavior
- Verbal communication skills
- Effective listening skills
- Enthusiasm and energy
- Flexibility and adaptability
- Imagination, creativity, and resourcefulness
- Positive attitude
- Honesty
- Sincerity
- Alertness and attentiveness
- Thoughtfulness
- Persuasiveness
- Poise
- Logical and well-organized thinking

As you review this list, you will notice that the professional competence of a person is not included. What that indicates is that it is a given that you are good, that you are qualified. Your resumé should attest to this and you should be able to convince the interviewer. The traits listed above are those personal/professional characteristics which determine if you fit in, if you are the right person for the job and, therefore, one who should be offered the job.

One interviewer summed it up by saying that he looks for "presence" in a job candidate, a quality which indicates that the applicant is aware of the job and how he or she has the confidence to be the best person to do it.

You might say that in a half-hour interview no one could possibly detect all of the above qualities and others as well. But you would be surprised at how many of these qualities quickly come to the surface in a brief interchange of ideas. And remember that an interviewer is looking for those *particular* qualities. How you look and what you say may not be the only index to your personality and your qualifications, but this is the only opportunity your interviewer has to find out.

The intangible qualities of sincerity, poise, alertness, and thoughtfulness cannot easily be analyzed. It is usually a combination of elements such as posture, reaction, and attitude in general that creates a personal dynamic or chemistry that will sell you as an applicant.

No one wants to hire a negative, pessimistic person, no matter how impressive his or her credentials. On the other hand, you harm yourself if you try to develop an unnatural or flamboyant personality. What you must do is to recognize your own style, try to eliminate your personal weaknesses, and develop your unique strengths. It all comes down to learning how to be confident in yourself and developing the skills to convey this confidence.

Here are some tips for a successful interview:

- Develop a good, firm handshake.

- Avoid stammering. It is far better to indicate that you would like to think about the answer to a question if you do not know it.

- Observe your interviewer's interests and background. You may want to use some of this information in your follow-up letter.

- Listen. Try to find out what happened to the last person in this position, which can be an indication of how rapid the turnover is — unless it is a new position. Find out about the company's method of handling finances, budgetary policies, and any other details that pertain to the job you want.

- Have questions prepared to fill in gaps of long silence. Later in this chapter is a list of questions you could have on hand. It is perfectly acceptable to come prepared with a small notebook which includes your questions or questions you might jot down during the interview. Use good judgment and avoid being conspicuous if you do so.

- Interest and enthusiasm are important, but no matter how much you want the job, it is generally unwise to accept any offer, no matter how attractive it looks, on the spur of the moment. An employer will not rescind the offer if you request some time (a few days or a week at the most) to think about it. That will give you time to think over any questions you may have.

  On the other hand, do not hesitate to ask, at the end of the interview, what time limit they have set on making their decision for hiring.

Finally, here are some things you should *avoid* in an interview:

- Do not arrive late. Plan to be ten to fifteen minutes early. Any earlier can make you appear overly anxious.

- Leave your packages and outerwear in the outer office. There is usually a closet or coat rack area for this purpose.

- Never apologize for your lack of experience or credentials, or for what you may perceive as your liabilities.

- Do not chew gum or mints. Do not smoke.

- Avoid negative comments on a past employer or organization. Avoid discussions of a personal or potentially volatile nature, such as race, politics, religion, or feminist issues.

- Do not lose your temper. If you do not agree with the interviewer's point of view, remember that you are under no obligation to accept the job or to work for this organization. You want to leave the interviewer with the best impression of you.

- Do not sermonize or overpower the conversation in an effort to sell yourself. It is easy to oversell and lose the job.

- Be courteous, but not effusive or insincere.

- Do not call the interviewer by his or her first name. On the other hand, avoid "sir" and "ma'am." Those words put you in too much of a subordinate position.

- Do not wear sunglasses. An interviewer will want eye contact.

- Do not tap on the desk, jingle change, or display any other nervous manifestations. If you are aware of these habits when you are nervous, try to control them by being conscious of them.

- Do not look at your watch. Try to observe the interviewer and let him or her set the pace of the interview.

- Do not ask, "Will I get the job?" or "Can I have the job?" Rather, state, "I hope that you will consider me as a candidate. I really am interested."

- Do not ask about salary until later on in the hiring process, perhaps at a second interview. The interviewer will generally bring it up. If it is brought up immediately in the first interview, simply postpone the discussion by indicating that you would like to first know more about the position and what it entails.

- Although you want to project self-confidence, be careful of sounding too cocky. Be realistic about your talents and qualifications, but a touch of modesty helps.

- Do not be evasive. If a question is too personal, indicate that you feel that it is, but that perhaps you misinterpreted what the interviewer was asking. Then change the topic.

Later on in this chapter, a list of illegal or discriminatory questions is included. If you are asked these questions, you should try to give a general reply which will reveal your professionalism. If you confront the interviewer with the illegality of the question, it may become unpleasant. Remember that you do not need to accept such a position. It is far better to be graceful and professional.

- Do not hesitate to ask questions you may have about the job. You might prepare a brief list. It will impress the interviewer that you have thought about the job and company before coming in.

Following is a list of such questions as well as questions *you* might be asked.

Questions You May Be Asked During an Interview

Tell me something about yourself.
Why did you decide to become a paralegal?
What made you change fields?
Why do you think you'd like to work for us?
What's important to you in a job?
What do you think determines a person's progress
   in a company?
How do you feel about traveling on the job?
What about working overtime and weekends?
What are your own special abilities and skills?
What is your major weakness?
What is your greatest strength?
Can you take instructions without getting upset?
Do you like to work individually or alone?
What type of boss do you prefer?
Have you ever had any difficulties getting along with
   your bosses?
How do you like routine work?
How do you feel about typing?
Are you a detailed person?
What motivates you in a job?
Where do you think you'd like to be five years from now?
Are you interested in going to law school?
How would you describe yourself, if you were another
   person talking about you?
You seem to be overqualified. Do you think you would be
   happy in this job?

Questions You May Ask

Is this a new position?
If so, why is this position needed?
If not, how long was the last person in the position?
Why did they leave?
To whom do I report?
Will I be working for more than one attorney?
Are paralegals in this firm considered part of the professional staff?
Is clerical help available?
What are the job's major responsibilities?
Will I have an opportunity to meet with other paralegals currently working in your firm?
Does your firm encourage continuing education and professional development?
What major problems would I encounter on this job?
When do you think you will be making your hiring decision?

List your own special interests, concerns, or questions you have about the job:

_____

_____

_____

_____

_____

_____

_____

_____

Difficult Questions You May Be Asked During the Interview and How to Handle Them

Federal regulations prohibit an interviewer from asking any questions which indicate a discrimination in the hiring process. This does not mean that these questions will not crop up in some form. Be prepared, therefore, to answer these questions in a way that will serve you best.

For example, if an interviewer asks you about your family responsibilities and care of your small children, should you have any, make certain that you convey that you have already prepared for their care should any problem arise. The same holds true if you are asked about your marital status or your plans for having a family. Make your answer brief, but focus on the importance of your professional commitment at this point.

If questions arise about your willingness, availability for travel or overtime (if that is a part of the job), again stress how you (and your spouse, family, etc.) have thought through the situation and have planned that it would be possible for you, providing you have sufficient notice for any extraordinary circumstances.

Any questions about your spouse's profession, salary, interests, or career goals should be shaped into answers that divulge the minimum amount of information.

The more you can anticipate difficult questions and prepare for them, the more your anxieties will be alleviated before going into the interview.

What would be the most difficult question for *you* to answer? One that you hope will not be asked? Plan on how you would answer such a question. If you are not asked, the issue is irrelevant. If you are asked, at least you have considered how you could answer it.

For example: Are you concerned about long gaps between employment? If so, think about how you have kept yourself abreast of current issues, have worked in various (non-paid) positions, attended workshops, continuing education programs, and so forth.

Do you feel that age is a factor for you? Think of all you can bring to a job: maturity, reliability, good judgment, an awareness of people, the ability to handle conflicts. In other words, once you convince yourself you could be an asset to a firm, you can convince an employer with much greater ease.

Responses to Difficult Questions

The previous information summarizes how to prepare yourself for handling difficult questions. Following are some specific ways in which you can protect yourself without alienating the interviewer who poses some questions which are illegal or border on illegality. Take your clues from these answers as you prepare your own answers.

Q: Do you plan to have a family? (Men are generally not asked this question.)

A: My husband and I are both committed to my new full-time job and currently we have planned to postpone our family. I want to be able to keep my time flexible at this stage in my career.

Q: What will you do if your children become ill? (If it has been established that you already have a family.)

A: Although my children (son/daughter) have a history of good health and regular check-ups, if they suddenly require medical attention, I have made arrangements with (spouse, friend, neighbor, relative, etc.) to be on call. In an emergency, of course, I would have to make contingent plans, but I have established a reliable support system.

Working Overtime/Travel

Q: How does your spouse feel about your working overtime/traveling?

A: We have already discussed the possibility of my working irregular hours and have agreed that our schedule is flexible enough to handle what the job requires. Of course, it's always easier if I have advance notice, just to make any necessary arrangements or reschedule something. *Traveling*: depending upon the amount of time involved, I don't have any problem with traveling if I can plan ahead.

Age Issues

(Note: The age issue may come up in many forms. The basic question being asked here is: "Are you too old to handle this job?")

Q: How do you feel about working for younger people?

A: (Depending upon context of question): I've been around young people for most of my life, particularly my own children, and I've not only learned from them, but I've developed a respect for them. I know I can bring that ability to this job, whatever the age of my supervisor or boss. Age is never a barrier, as far as I'm concerned. It's the person's attitude toward age and how well he or she gets along with people.

These are just some examples of how to approach difficult questions. Now list the toughest questions you think you might be asked and prepare the questions. You are readying yourself for a successful interview.

Federal Laws and Regulations Concerning Discrimination in Employment

1. Executive Order 11246, amended by 11375, prohibits discrimination in employment practices (hiring, promotions, benefits, training, salaries) on the basis of race, color, religion, national origin, or sex for all the employers with federal contracts over ten thousand dollars. Report violations to Office of Federal Contract Compliance of the Department of Labor, Washington, D.C. 20210.

2. Age Discrimination in Employment Act prohibits discrimination in employment practices (hiring, salaries, discharge). Report violations to the Wage and Hour Division of the Employment Standards Administration of the Department of Labor, Washington, D.C. 20210.

3. Title VII of the Civil Rights Act prohibits discrimination in employment practices on the basis of race, color, national origin, sex, or religion for all employers with fifteen or more employees. Report violations to Equal Employment Opportunity Commission, 1800 G Street NE, Washington, D.C. 20506.

4. Equal Pay Act prohibits discrimination in salaries, including most fringe benefits, on the basis of sex. Report violations to Wage and Hour Division of the Employment Standards Administration, Department of Labor, Washington, D.C. 20210.

Discriminatory Practices on Application Forms or During Interview

1. Questions concerning applicant's race, religious affiliation, birthplace, or birthplace of applicant's parents.

2. Requirement that applicant submit birth certificate, naturalization, or baptismal record.*

3. Photographs with application. After hiring, a photograph may be required for identification purposes.

4. Date of birth or age of applicant, unless such information is needed to meet minimum age requirements.

5. Questions concerning applicant's mother tongue or language commonly used by applicant at home.

6. Inquiries about applicant's military experience in other than U.S. Armed Forces.

7. Draft status of applicant may not be asked, although it is legal to ask whether applicant has received any notice to report for duty in the Armed Forces.

*It is no longer discriminatory to require such proof once an applicant is hired, since recent federal immigration laws require employers to document U.S. citizenship for employment eligibility.

8. Questions about applicant's memberships in any organizations other than professional, trade, or service organizations.

9. Arrest record information (although conviction record may be requested).

10. Inquiries about relatives, except who should be notified in emergencies.

11. Marital status, number of children, or plans for a family.

Salary Negotiations

The question of salary is undoubtedly one of the most delicate points that you have to negotiate, but inevitably it will come up, and you must be prepared to bargain for what you feel you are worth and feel that you can get.

If at all possible, the discussion of salary and other employee benefits should be delayed until a job offer has been made, or at least until it has been made clear to you that you are being considered very seriously. Obviously, this can happen only after the interviewer has had an opportunity to talk with you or even call you in for a second interview.

If the question comes up early in the interview (such as, "What is the minimum salary you will accept?"), your best strategy is to use some kind of delaying tactic. For example, you could reply, "That's difficult to answer right now. It would depend on the job and its responsibilities, and I'd like to know more before I can answer."

The purpose of postponing salary discussion is so you can impress your interviewer with your presentation of yourself. Eventually, however, if both of you establish a mutual interest, you will have to confront the salary issue. And the more you know about salary ranges offered by this particular company, as well as salary ranges for paralegals in the area, the better prepared you are to discuss this topic.

Before the interview is the time to do your salary investigation, not *during* the interview. You cannot negotiate until you have some idea of what the general range is in the field. You must also know your own minimum requirements as well. Otherwise, you waste your time if the company cannot pay what you need to earn. Salary scales are generally not available, but you can gain information on ranges from a paralegal association in the area in which you want to work.

If there is a range within a company, bargain for the top of the range; the company wants you to agree on the lower part of the range. With persuasion on your part of what you have to offer the organization, the idea is for you to agree on what is mutually acceptable. If the salary is fixed, however (and ask if the salary offered you is a firm one), then ask what other benefits are available and when you have a salary review. Doing so demonstrates your ambition as well as initiative. Finally, only you can decide on what salary is fair and acceptable to you. Again, doing your homework is essential before you can make a decision.

Closing the Interview and Planning Your Follow-up

Generally, you have some clues when the interview is over. The interviewer either stands or asks if you have any questions about the job. That is your chance to ask questions you did not have an opportunity to ask earlier, but even more important, it is the time for you to appraise how well you did if you are interested in the job.

The interviewer may offer definite feedback by the type of comments or questions he or she asks. That may take the form of planning the next step. If that does not happen, try to get some indication of your possible chances for the job. You can do this easily without appearing brash. For example, if you have no clue from the interviewer, you can simply ask, "Is there anything more about my background or experience you would like to know, as it relates to this job?" Or "Do I seem to have the kind of experience that you're looking for?" These kinds of questions can elicit either favorable comments, negative ones, or noncommittal ones. If there is not a definite interest exhibited at this point, you can support your case in the follow-up letter.

Whatever the outcome of the interview, your follow-up letter marks you as a professional who is also courteous. Try to remember the interests and needs of the employer and refer to them in the letter, stressing again how you feel qualified for the job and would enjoy working for the organization now that you have had an opportunity to find out more about it. Keep the letter brief, but be sure to end it on the note that you look forward to hearing from the interviewer concerning the position. Model letters are included at the end of this chapter.

You will hear, one way or the other. If the interviewer is interested, you may be called in for a second interview, particularly if salary negotiations were not finalized. A phone call from the company is always a good sign, although it may not mean that the job is definite. Regrets and rejections always come in the form of a letter, sometimes weeks after the job is filled.

If you are interested in the job, however, and wrote your courtesy letter after the interview, call the company within a week or so to see if they made their decision or when they expect to make it. Other than that, your best course of action is to review all the steps you have taken and analyze your interview.

One of the best ways for you to evaluate your performance in your interviews is to keep a log and record of your reactions as soon after the interview as possible. The following model will help you to keep this record and evaluate yourself. Doing so may help you to improve your interviewing skills with practice and experience.

Job Search Log

Name of Firm Address, Phone	Interviewer's Name Title	Interview Date	Follow-up Date	Comments

Interview Log
Self-Evaluation Chart

Interview Date	Name of Firm	Positive Points	Negative Points

Some points you may wish to include are given below. Add your own points to the list.

Positive Points:
> Good chemistry with interviewer
> Congenial atmosphere
> Answered questions confidently, directly
> Interviewer seemed to focus on my strengths
> Job described clearly

Negative Points:
> Interviewer not interested
> Forgot to bring up important information
> Felt uncomfortable and nervous
> Felt rushed in answering
> Did not feel comfortable about appearance
> Was late for appointment
> Did not understand questions asked
> Lacked confidence

The purpose of this self-evaluation is so you can recognize your weaknesses and overcome them as you continue the interviewing process. Make extra sheets for each interview. It is helpful for you to keep a log of your job contacts: the action taken and the results. Remember to send a note of acknowledgement to these contacts. Your courtesy reflects your professionalism. These brief notes (typed) should also indicate the results of any leads given.

Job Contact Log

Name of Contact, Firm, Address, Phone	Action Taken/Results	Date Acknowledgement Sent

5643 Riverside Drive
Berwyn, IL 60402
December 4, 1991

Mr. Dean McCoy
McCoy Legal Associates
555 Wacker Drive
Chicago, IL 60601

Dear Mr. McCoy:

I appreciate the time you took from your busy schedule to discuss future job opportunities as a paralegal with McCoy Legal Associates. Although you do not presently have any paralegals on your staff, I hope that in the very near future you will find it beneficial to do so.

When that happens, I hope that you will keep me in mind. I enjoyed our meeting and would look forward to working with you.

Sincerely yours,

Margaret Ivetic

3211 S. 52nd Court
Cicero, IL 60650
August 26, 1991

Ms. Martha Haney
Rowland & Allen Law Associates
555 N. Michigan Avenue
Chicago, IL 60601

Dear Ms. Haney:

After our brief meeting the other day, I reviewed our discussion and realized what a good match my skills would be with Rowland & Allen Law Associates. I appreciate your time, interest, and helpful suggestions about paralegal career opportunities in general. Should an opening occur within your firm, I would, of course, be grateful to hear about it.

Again, thank you for taking the time out of your busy schedule to meet with me. I hope we have an opportunity to see each other again.

Sincerely yours,

Andrew Jefferson

Follow-up Letters

7

A day or so after the interview has taken place, write a brief follow-up letter to the person or persons who interviewed you. In doing so, you not only impress the interviewer with your courtesy, you remind him or her of how much you are really interested in the position, and how well-qualified you are to fill it. The letter should be brief, typed, and reiterate what you believe are your strengths, as well as your suitability for the position. Some of the following letters illustrate how you can easily focus these points.

Again, write individual letters and customize your correspondence to the specific interviewer and job.

Follow-up letters take a little time and care, but if you are willing to put forth the effort, you may well be ahead of the majority of those interviewed who do not send such a letter.

The samples are brief, to the point, and cover the variety of responses you might want to send.

Below are some guidelines for your follow-up letter:

1. Thank the person or persons who interviewed you for their interest and valuable time.

2. If possible, refer to some part of the personal conversation (shared interests, goals, and so forth).

3. Express your enthusiasm for the position.

4. Reinforce your strengths and why you think you are particularly suited for the position.

5. If certain liabilities were brought up in the interview, be sure to address how you can compensate for any weaknesses by the strengths you bring to the job (such as a lack of experience in the specifics of the job and how your experience in your past jobs could make you an asset to the firm).

6. Refer to the next step in the process: "I look forward to hearing from you soon about your decision."

If you get the job, send an acceptance letter to confirm the starting date and time. Even if you did not get the job, a follow-up letter demonstrates a true professional attitude.

2800 Orchard
Chicago, IL 60604
October 30, 1991

Mr. Wayne Smith
Prince Products
1822 W. Madison
Chicago, IL 60607

Dear Mr. Smith:

It was a pleasure meeting you today to discuss the job opening in the paralegal department of Prince Products.

The position seems to be an opportunity for me to use my background and training in a stimulating environment. In reviewing the plans for your company's growth, I am even more enthusiastic about the contributions I can make as a paralegal.

Again, I did appreciate the opportunity to talk with you, and hope that we will be working together in the future.

Sincerely,

Mark Harrison

9823 S. Hamlin
Des Plaines, IL 60016
August 2, 1991

Mr. John Downey
Wentworth, Katz & Walter Associates
One N. Dearborn Street
Chicago, IL 60602

Dear Mr. Downey:

Thank you for the opportunity to discuss the paralegal opening at Wentworth, Katz & Walter Associates. I enjoyed discussing the company's present commitment and future plans. It is a lively and challenging work environment and I know that I could bring valuable business experience and skills to the position.

I hope that we will be working together in the future and I look forward to hearing from you sometime soon.

Sincerely,

Felicia Simmons

1255 W. 51st Street
Downers Grove, IL 60516
November 9, 1991

Mr. Harold Henderson
Henderson Law Associates
212 W. Wesley St
Wheaton, IL 60187

Dear Mr. Henderson:

I just wanted to let you know how pleased I am to be invited to join Henderson Law Associates as a paralegal.

The day you suggested, May 15, is a perfect starting date and I will report to you and Mr. Simpson at 9:00 a.m. in the first floor conference room.

In the meantime, thank you for this opportunity to begin my paralegal career with such a prestigious firm. I look forward to making a contribution at Henderson Law Associates.

Sincerely,

Marcia Morgan

600 Mulberry
Highland Park, IL 60035
December 18, 1991

Mrs. Judith Royce
Vice-President
First National Bank of Lombard
Lombard, IL 60157

Dear Mrs. Royce:

I am truly sorry things did not work out for me at First National Bank. However, I must say it was a pleasure to meet you, and I thank you for all the time you spent with me discussing career opportunities in the paralegal department at First National.

Should you hear of any positions that become available and seem to suit my background and experience, I would appreciate hearing from you. Again, many thanks for your interest.

Sincerely,

Thomas Ferguson

932 Ash Street
Winnetka, IL 60093
October 29, 1991

Mr. Frederic Bates
Midwest Agronomy Corporation
Wilkins Boulevard
Naperville, IL 60180

Dear Mr. Bates:

I received your letter on Thursday with the disappointing news that the Midwest Agronomy Corporation was not pursuing opportunities with me further. The reason I am writing is to ask if this decision might be reconsidered.

In my research of Midwest Agronomy, I was convinced that my background and interests, along with my credentials as a paralegal, seemed to be a perfect match. A visit to the firm further impressed this point upon me. The stimulating environment as well as dedicated staff create a challenging atmosphere — one in which I would feel privileged to work.

If this request for reconsideration seems unusual, I hope you'll understand it is because I would very much like to be a part of Midwest Agronomy and I feel that I could make a substantial contribution to the organization. I look forward to hearing from you again.

Sincerely yours,

Alexander B. Martin

Some Final Thoughts on Your Job Search

After you complete each chapter of this book, the final, most important step still lies ahead: developing a plan for your job search campaign. For unless you have a well thought out strategy, you may easily become frustrated or disillusioned. But, how do you begin?

Your job search plan should include the following:

1. *Your objectives*

   What type of employer are you looking for? Include size of organization, location, type of work specialty (if relevant), and any other details that help you to focus on the kind of job you would like to have. It is not essential for you to limit your options, but the clearer you are in your objectives, the easier it is for you to make a job search plan.

   The list of paralegal employers in the Appendix also proves helpful at this stage.

2. *Your resources*

   List reference materials you plan to use. (See Appendix.)

   List personal contacts you plan to use.
   Everyone you know should be aware that you are looking for a job. The discussion on networking which follows explains how you can widen your range of contacts, but begin by listing all your friends, relatives, and friends of relatives who might be able to help you.

   Other job sources should include:
   Alumni offices and career centers of schools you have attended
   Local bulletin boards and professional newsletters of community and civic organizations
   Job fairs
   Professional association meetings
   Yellow pages
   Classified ads
   The "hidden job market," opportunities which exist but which are not advertised. These could be the result of events such as a merger, expansion, or someone leaving. The best inside track to the hidden job market is through networking.
   Add your other job sources to this list.

3. *Your record-keeping system*

   This should include a log of job contacts, networking contacts, interviews, follow-ups, expenses, and so forth. Charts in this book provide samples on how to set up your records.

Networking

Within recent years, the concept of *networking* has become increasingly popular as it relates to job finding, career counseling, and support systems. To understand how networking operates, visualize a series of linkages or connections that lead to other connections. That's what networking is all about: developing connections or contacts who might be able to open some doors for you in your job search.

You are probably familiar with the system referred to as the "old boys' network," in which job information is shared over lunch, on the golf course, at a party. It's an informal way of discussing what's going on from an insider's vantage point before such information is available to the general public. It's also a system of strategies whereby someone who knows a person within an organization can make a phone call or set up an introduction for you.

When you think of it, everyone is at the core of a network of friends or associates. In your job search, you learn how to expand your network. You can do this in a number of ways. Professional associations, such as the paralegal associations mentioned in the Appendix, meet regularly. Attending a meeting helps you to meet others in the field to find out about job opportunities, as well as other important information: What are the working conditions like within a company? What are the promotion policies? What are current salary ranges? And much more.

It takes energy and initiative to attend such meetings or similar ones such as job fairs, lectures or special programs, but the investment of your time is well worth it. You must learn how to put yourself forward, strike up a conversation, or simply listen until you have something to contribute. As you develop a rapport and trust with others, information that is not otherwise discussed becomes easier to talk about and share.

Sometimes networking can take the shape of a casual lunch in which you meet a new person, a friend of a mutual friend. It can take place at a formal party or picnic. All of these occasions provide opportunities for you to develop and expand your connections. If you are not convinced, just take time at a social gathering to watch how people congregate to talk about work-related issues and problems. Work is frequently the common denominator in a discussion; work is frequently what brings people together, even socially. Observe how others use networking as an effective strategy and then learn how to do it yourself.

It's important to remember, however, that networking is not manipulation or using other people. Everyone must gain something from it; otherwise, it does not work. You must reciprocate in some fashion. Always send a thank you note and if you are offered a job contact, follow through with an acknowledgement note to the person who made the connection for you and let that person know the result of your meeting.

Another strategy is to follow up with materials of interest to the other person: a newspaper clipping, a magazine article, or an upcoming event announcement. Such behavior marks you as a professional and your name will come to mind when others hear of job openings.

Networking will not get you the job, but it will expand your professional circle and it could help you meet the right person.

Employment Agencies

Should you use an employment agency to find a job? Recently, a number of employment agencies opened to primarily handle paralegal placement. Check the yellow pages as well as the classified ads in professional journals. Make certain that the agency does not view paralegals as secretaries with a little extra training. Also, read any agency contract before signing so that you understand the fees involved. The best agency reference will be someone who has used and been satisfied with the services of the agency.

Free-lancing

Finally, you may have thought of free-lancing as a paralegal. The following chapter discusses what you need to know about that career option if you decide to pursue that route now or at some time in the future.

Free-lancing As a Paralegal

8

Many paralegals, once they gain experience and establish a reputation of reliability and professional work, consider free-lancing — working as independent contractors or with other paralegals as part of a group.

This section explains the qualifications for becoming a free-lance paralegal and some of the marketing strategies necessary for success in this independent venture.

First of all, there are two types of free-lance paralegals. The first is generally referred to as an *independent contractor.* This type of paralegal is not on the payroll of any one organization, but works independently and bills his or her services to an attorney or law firm. Independent contractors usually bill their clients on an hourly basis, but at times will contract for a specific project on a fixed rate for the entire project.

Frequently, these paralegals work out of their homes and work many areas of legal service. They often maintain a post office box address to maintain a professional image.

The second type of free-lance paralegal is a *service group paralegal,* one who works as part of a service company. Paralegal service companies generally have their own office space, have a staff of clerical help, and may offer specialized services, such as in trusts and estates. Essentially, these groups are made up of entrepreneurs who need to be good business managers as well as knowledgeable paralegals.

Both the independent contractor paralegal and the service group paralegal bill their clients on an hourly basis, depending upon the complexity of the work involved.

While there may seem to be a specific advantage in becoming a free-lance paralegal, it is not easy to become a successful one. First, you must understand the qualifications you need — in addition to your paralegal training. Then you must develop a marketing strategy to sell your services.

Qualifications

To be qualified to offer paralegal services, you need credentials and experience. Only by training and professional experience will you gain the necessary expertise to convince a client to buy your service. That client will want to know your background, what you have done, and how your former clients feel about your work. For these reasons, you should have several years of experience, from four to five years, before trying your hand as a free-lancing paralegal. For simple, routine tasks, a shorter time will suffice.

Once you gain experience, you not only develop a certain expertise, but have a level of self-confidence necessary to getting started and marketing your services.

In addition to the professional qualifications, you need certain personal qualifications for success as a free-lance paralegal. You need a commitment to long, irregular hours, strong interpersonal communication skills, and the ability to work under varying deadlines and in pressure situations.

Remember that your first clients are the ones who will help you to establish your reputation. You cannot afford to be anything less than punctual and completely accurate in the work you do. While these traits are important in any job, as an independent paralegal you will never hold clients or gain new ones if your reputation is not built on these factors.

How much start-up money will you need? You won't need a lot of capital to begin your free-lancing career, but the expenses you need to meet include: stationery, business cards, a basic brochure, a mailing list, and an answering service or machine. Remember that you are establishing yourself and your reputation, so be certain that you invest in quality items in any materials advertising your new business. Your stationery and business cards need not be elaborate, but they must project a professional image.

Many free-lancers work part-time for someone else until they develop their own clientele. And this comes to a very important issue which we will address later, that is, conflict of interests.

A final qualification which serves you well as a free-lancer is the development of your selling skills. You are selling a service, as well as yourself. But in order for someone to buy your product, you must know how to present it. A good speaking or presentation skills course and constant practice will prove very helpful to you, particularly before you approach your first clients.

In a competitive marketplace, you gain the edge over other free-lancing paralegals if you develop a specialty and gain as much experience as you can in your specialty. In doing so, you can develop a reputation as a qualified and skilled paralegal and build your clientele by good, strong referrals.

There are other important things to consider when being a paralegal free-lancer.

Getting Paid

As a free-lancer, you must learn how and when to bill your clients. One of the most difficult aspects of working for yourself is collecting money for services you have performed. For that reason, it is essential that you remember some basic points:

- Explain to your clients your fees and make certain that you agree upon what your reimbursement will be. Confirm this agreement *in writing* so there is no dispute later on or any confusion about the terms you stipulated.

- Whether you decide to bill on an hourly basis (and you can check either in your community or with your local paralegal association to find out the going rate), or charge a flat fee for a specific project, be certain to bill your clients promptly. For lengthy projects, it is wise to bill regularly, every week or two. For a shorter project, send your bill within two weeks of completion of your work.

Ethical Responsibilities

- Avoid conflict of interest situations. If you work for several law firms that specialize in the same area, you may find that you are working for opposing sides of a case. If you are uncertain, ask the attorneys for whom you will be working whether they feel that your working for both clients would constitute a conflict. If so, it is your ethical responsibility to act accordingly, particularly if you are working in a litigation case.

- It is important to remember that while the duties and responsibilities of a paralegal are diverse, a paralegal is not a lawyer and you may not offer legal advice to a non-lawyer client. You may not represent a client in court and you may not advertise your services as those of a lawyer.

In order to protect yourself from any possibility of infringement on these laws, it is best to take some precautions by following these guidelines:

- Never work directly for the general public. Always work for an attorney.

- Do not meet independently with a client of an attorney.

- Make certain that the attorney for whom you are working reviews and signs your work.

- Have the attorney for whom you work give you a letter which authorizes you to perform certain duties for him or her.

- Be sure that the attorney for whom you are working has been admitted to practice law in your state.

Keep abreast of problems which have faced other free-lance paralegals and learn how they have solved them. Become familiar with your local paralegal association, not only for job opportunities which may exist, but to find out how to enhance your professional status as a paralegal within the community, whether you decide to work independently, as a free-lancer, or within an organization as a full-time paralegal.

Finally, here are some helpful hints and suggestions on becoming a successful free-lancer from Jean Hellman, Director of the Institute for Paralegal Studies at Loyola University, Chicago, Illinois.

- First, it is essential to keep accurate, up-to-date records of all income and expenses. Formal bookkeeping isn't required, but you must have a system. Keep your check stubs or make copies of paychecks before depositing them; collect receipts for supplies and the like. Consider a separate checking account for your business, and maybe even a separate phone line if you are working from your home.

- Second, consider the legal aspects of doing business on your own. If you are asked to sign a contract, read it carefully and make sure you understand every word first. If you're uncertain, get legal advice; it shouldn't cost much and will be well worth it to prevent problems later.

- Finally, realize the tax consequences of free-lancing. If your employer is not withholding taxes, you may have to make estimated tax payments quarterly and pay Social Security taxes when you file your annual return; if you don't, you may be penalized by the IRS. Again, tax advice is relatively inexpensive. A good tax advisor will also be able to tell you of deductions you may take against your business income (even under the new tax laws). This is another reason why your record keeping is so important.

While free-lancing as a paralegal may appear to be complicated, the rewards can be great. Only you can decide the route you wish to follow. As in any decision, the more you understand about the implications and the consequences, the easier it may be for you to choose the option which is best for you.

In order to make the maximum use of your time and monetary investment, you need to establish efficient systems for your calendar, billing, telephones, filing, references, and resources. The following checklist may be helpful in the beginning.

Sample Checklist for Free-lancing
(You may wish to duplicate this for monthly items.)

Expense Sheet

Item	Amount	Date
Stationery		
Business Cards		
Contracts		
Postage		
Supplies (list)		
Travel Expenses		
Telephone		
Office Equipment (list)		
Professional Dues/Memberships		
Other		

Income Sheet

Received From	Payment For	Date	Amount	Balance Due

Paralegal: Stepping Stone to Other Careers

9

As you begin your career as a paralegal, you will probably not be interested in seeing how your training can prepare you for jobs and careers outside the legal field. Sometime later, however, you might find such information useful. It is very helpful, therefore, to consider these options as you proceed, even from the beginning. For what you will realize is that your education and training as a paralegal may well serve as a stepping stone to other areas which may be of interest to you.

In the beginning of this book, we discussed what it takes to become a successful paralegal. Many of the qualifications listed are the same qualifications it takes to be successful in several fields or professions. With the professional training of a paralegal, you may wish to explore some of the fields once you gain some experience.

Most of you have trained in other fields before becoming a paralegal. As a matter of fact, one of the problems many people face as they begin this new career is how to explain what might be a radical career change to a potential employer. If you can learn how to build on your skills developed in another field and relate these skills to your paralegal training, then you will benefit from the broad range of your talents and experiences, rather than be at a disadvantage.

Eventually, you may find that you use this combination of skills and training if you wish to move on to another field. Consider the following examples:

- Depending upon your specific interests and talents, you can make many moves within the paralegal profession, as well as outside of it.

- Management skills could enable you to become a paralegal coordinator, one who trains and supervises other paralegals within an organization. The best route to this position is within an organization, once your capabilities have been demonstrated.

- Office management is another area in which you can use management and supervisory skills. This could be within a legal firm or, once you have gained experience, you may find that many offices need good management, outside as well as inside the legal profession.

- Administration within a legal firm is also based on strong skills in working with personnel of many departments. An administrative director of a law firm is generally responsible for every non-legal aspect of the firm's operation, including accounting, personnel, purchasing, etc.

    This person usually reports to a senior officer. It is a highly responsible and demanding position. Someone with a paralegal background and other administrative skills could find this a rewarding and challenging position.

Within large, small, non-profit, and corporate environments, paralegals could find opportunities as:

- Computer Center Specialist/Manager

    Computer literacy training, in addition to specialized or generalist training, could make you a suitable candidate for a position as a computer center manager. While duties may vary, they would include working with information systems, electronic data banks, word processing, etc. Anyone with computer skills in addition to paralegal training could find this a satisfying career alternative.

- Law Librarian

    Law firms generally hire law librarians to handle their periodical collections, as well as law books and manuals. Although many of these law positions are filled by those with library training, frequently a paralegal with a good academic background can be trained to fill this position.

    Other specific fields that should be explored by paralegals, for all facets of legal work, include: banking, importing and exporting, stock brokerage, journalism (research and writing in the legal field), sales (for all materials and equipment used by attorneys), real estate, teaching/program administration, lobbying, employee benefits, insurance (investigation, adjustive), and corporate specialties (trademark, patents, etc.).

While each of these fields might require additional training (not necessarily a degree, but some specialized training that could be gained on the job), they should be considered, particularly if they seem to tie in with your interests and talents.

You may, of course, plan to go on to law school, but the point of this discussion is to emphasize that becoming a paralegal can lead you to job opportunities in many different fields, some directly related and others indirectly related to the legal field.

Additional educational training might be necessary should you wish to become an expert in the field. That may not always be the case. For example, you may not be certain where your true interests and talents lie; so until you do, going ahead with additional education or training may not be the answer. Being a paralegal will give you a good idea of what it would be like to remain in the legal field should you decide you want to become a lawyer. But even if you do not wish to do so, think of your paralegal training as a background for developing other interests you have. It's also important to realize that being a paralegal could easily be a stepping stone to other careers, careers which are not as rigorous and demanding as that of a paralegal — or perhaps even more so, but in a different way. There may be other areas in which you could expand your talents and professional options.

In considering your professional development as a paralegal or in other fields, review the list of resources in the Appendix of this book to help you as you make your plans.

- Develop special interests and expertise in the area of law that appeals to you.

- Continue your professional education — become involved with your local paralegal association and attend professional workshops and programs that will help you develop your skills and let you know about your options.

- Develop your networking affiliations. Let people know of your interests and ambitions. Don't forget to thank them when they have helped you in any way.

- Look for ways to become the best at what you do and gain visibility for your work.

- Remember that you should at least perform the job for which you are hired. If you become bored or burned out, it could be that you have not planned to take the next step. Always keep in mind that you do have options. Learn to discover them.

- Update your resumé periodically. Be prepared to submit a copy to someone who could be interested in what you have done.

- Learn to build on your past experiences and integrate them into the job you are doing or a position you would like to have.

- Take the time and effort to develop strong communication skills: interpersonal, written, and verbal.

- Find ways to use these skills so that you are recognized not only for what you do, but for what you are capable of doing.

Suggestions for Planning Your Future As a Paralegal

- Learn to set standards of excellence for yourself in your job without being a fanatic perfectionist and without judging the work of others. Know the job for which you are responsible and do it to the best of your ability.

- Develop a self-analytical approach to your job and yourself. In planning your future, determine what is important to you as a professional, learn to examine your options carefully, and learn what is necessary to take the steps you need to take to achieve your goal.

Appendix A: Resources

In all aspects of your job search, you will need a broad range of information on available resources. That is the purpose of this Appendix — to help you locate what you need to know in order to become well-informed and well-prepared.

All of the information included is current at the time of publication, but be certain to verify specific names, addresses, and phone numbers for any recent changes.

- Employers of Paralegals

- Directories, Publications

- Law Lists

    General

    Insurance

    Probate

- Legal Publications

- Associations

- Federal Job Information Centers

- Paralegal Associations in the United States

- Additional Sources of Job Leads

A large percentage of paralegals may choose to work in traditional law firms of varying sizes and specialties. Information on how to locate these companies is listed in this Appendix. In addition to these traditional firms which practice law, there are many other opportunities for paralegals who decide to use their skills in other settings. Following is a list of categories of paralegal employment.

Employers of Paralegals

- *Private law firms, legal clinics*

  Paralegal duties
  Office managers
  General legal administrators

- *Businesses*

  Corporations
  Banks/lending institutions
  Accounting firms
  Brokerage firms
  Insurance companies
  Mortgage/title companies

- *Special Interest Groups*

  Consumer affairs groups
  Business associations
  Civil Liberties Union
  Labor Unions
  Trade associations
  Citizen action groups
  Environmental protection groups
  Taxpayer associations

- *Consulting Firms, Service Organizations*

  Trademark searches
  Billing services
  Branch office establishment
  Computer systems selection

- *Educational Institutions*

  Paralegal programs
      Administration
      Admissions
      Placement
      Paralegal training
      Internship coordination
  Law librarian

- *Government: Civil Service Departments*

  Federal Government
      Office of the chief government lawyer (attorney general,
      corporation counsel)
      General counsel's office of individual agencies
      Departments of individual agencies (civil rights division,
      enforcement department, etc.)

State/Local Government
 Offices of state and local politicians (governor, mayor, commissioner, alderman, representative, senator)
 Research assistant, legal analyst, administrative aide, administrative officer, executive assistant, investigator, examiner

Legal Services/Legal Aid Offices

Community legal service offices/legal aid offices providing services with the following titles:

Administrative Benefits Representative
Administrative Hearing Representative
AFDC Specialist (Aid to Families with Dependent Children)
Bankruptcy Law Specialist
Case Advocate
Community Education Specialist
Consumer Law Specialist
Disabled, Specialist in the Law of the
Domestic Relations Specialist
Employment Law Specialist
Generalist Paralegal
Health Law Specialist
Housing/Tenant Law Specialist
Immigrant Law Specialist
Information and Referral Specialist
Legal Research Specialist
Paralegal Coordinator
Public Entitlement Specialist
Senior Citizen Specialist
Social Security Specialist
Tribal Court Representative
Veterans Law Specialist
Wills Procedures Specialist

Directories, Publications

The American Law Guide (2 Park Avenue, New York)
Statistical and descriptive information on the top 200 law firms and major legal centers in the United States. Includes departments by size and specialty. Key clients and cases also listed.

Directory of Corporate Affiliations: "Who Owns Whom"

Directory of Directories (Gale Research Company, Detroit, Michigan)
A reference guide to directories in business, government, and public affairs. Includes useful section on specific areas, such as finance, banking, and real estate.

Land Trust Directory
Real estate magazine published by Law Bulletin Publishing Company.

The Law & Business Directory of Corporate Counsel (Law and Business Inc., Harcourt Brace Jovanovich, New York)
Listing of over 4500 companies, including utilities, insurance companies, and financial institutions. Names of attorneys with educational backgrounds, specialty, bar affiliation, and work experience. Geographical index included.

Lawyer's Register by Specialties and Field of Law (published annually by the Lawyer to Lawyer Consultation Panel, Inc., Cleveland)
National guide which lists attorneys by specialty with a section on corporate legal departments.

Martindale-Hubbell Law Directory (published annually by Martindale-Hubbell, Inc., Summit, New Jersey)
A listing of all attorneys admitted to the state bars in the United States, as well as some foreign attorneys. Listing is by states with three individual sections under each state: (1) attorneys and their law firms; (2) attorneys registered to practice before the U.S. Patent and Trademark Office; and (3) biographical directory of state law firms, listed by local address, including firm's specialties.

Million Dollar Directory
Information on over 120,000 U.S. businesses with a net worth of over $1,500,000. Geographical and specialty listing.

Moody's Manuals

Standard and Poor's (The Standard and Poor Company, New York)
Published semi-monthly with descriptions of publicly held corporations and their records. Names and titles of chief officers of each company are listed, with a description of the firm's major services or products. A separate volume lists all American executives with educational backgrounds. Index categorizes companies according to business specialty and geographical location.

Paralegal's Guide to U.S. Government Jobs

United States Government Manual
Listing of all federal government agencies and commissions with divisions and functions of each.

Other directories which could be helpful:

Encyclopedia of Associations (Gale Research Co., Detroit, Michigan)

National Trade and Professional Associations (Columbia Books, Inc., Washington, D.C.)

Literary Market Place (R.R. Bowker Co., New York and London)

The Writer's Market (Writer's Digest Books, Cincinnati, Ohio)

Both of these provide useful information for those interested in writing for publications on topics of interest to paralegals.

Law directories are available in most states and frequently on the city or county level.

General

American Bank Attorneys (Capron Publishing Corporation, Wellesley Hills, Massachusetts)

List of Lawyers for Motorists (Automobile Legal Association, Wellesley, Massachusetts)

Markham's Negligence Counsel (Markham Publishing Counsel, Stanford, Connecticut)

Motor Club of America Law List for Motorists (Motor Club of America, Newark, New Jersey)

Insurance

Best's Recommended Insurance Attorneys (Oldwick, New Jersey)

Hine's Insurance Counsel (Hine's Legal Directory, Inc., Glen Ellyn, Illinois)

The Insurance Bar (Bar List Publishing Co., Northfield, Illinois)

Underwriters List of Trial Counsel (Underwriters List Publication Co., Cincinnati, Ohio)

Probate

The Probate Counsel (Probate Counsel, Inc., Phoenix, Arizona)

Sullivan's Probate Directory, Inc. (Galesburg, Illinois)

American Bar Association Journal
Monthly news feature publication for lawyers. Special sections highlight current changes in the law. Classified ads for attorneys listed.

The American Lawyer
Profiles of current legal departments, major firms, client acquisitions, and significant cases. Also an annual in-depth survey of 100 major law firms.

Legal Assistant Today

The National Law Journal
Weekly newspaper which covers all aspects of law in the U.S., including classified ads.

Trial
Monthly journal for members of the Association of Trial Lawyers. Worth examining if you would like to consider working in this area.

Associations

Each region will have offices for the following associations. Check with your local paralegal association or your local telephone book for current addresses and telephone numbers. A space is given below for you to include this information which could be a valuable part of your job search.

Local Address/Phone Number

County Bar Association _____

_____ _____

American Bar Association _____

_____ _____

State Bar Association _____

_____ _____

Local Law Journals/Newspapers _____

_____ _____

_____ _____

_____ _____

Federal Job Information Centers

Federal Job Information Centers operated by the Office of Personnel Management can provide general information on how to apply for specific jobs and supply application materials. The Office of Personnel Management also provides federal employment information to state job service offices and to college placement offices. Many federal agencies also recruit directly for their own vacancies and provide a wide range of information services.

Alabama

Southerland Building
806 Governors Drive, N.W.
Huntsville, AL 35801
(205) 453-5070

Alaska

Federal Building & U.S. Courthouse
701 C Street
PO Box 22
Anchorage, AK 99513
(907) 271-5821

Arizona

522 North Central Avenue
Phoenix, AZ 85004
(602) 261-4736

Arkansas

Federal Building, Room 1319
700 West Capitol Avenue
Little Rock, AR 72201
(501) 378-5842

California

Linder Building
845 South Figueroa
Los Angeles, CA 90017
(213) 688-3360

Federal Building
650 Capitol Mall
Sacramento, CA 95814
(916) 440-3441

880 Front Street
San Diego, CA 92188
(714) 293-6165

Federal Building, Room 1001
450 Golden Avenue
San Francisco, CA 94102
(415) 556-6667

Colorado

1845 Sherman Street
Denver, CO 80203
(303) 837-3506

Connecticut

Federal Building, Room 717
450 Main Street
Hartford, CT 06103
(203) 244-3096

Delaware

Federal Building
844 King Street
Wilmington, DE 19801
(302) 571-6288

District of Columbia

1900 E Street, N.W.
Metro Area
Washington, DC 20415
(202) 737-9616

Florida

330 Biscayne Blvd., Suite 410
Miami, FL 33131
(305) 350-4725

80 N. Hughey Ave
Orlando, FL 32801
(305) 420-6148

Georgia

Richard B. Russell Federal Building
75 Spring St., S.W.
Atlanta, GA 30303
(404) 221-4315

Guam

238 O'Hara St.
Room 308
Agana, Guam 96910

Hawaii

Federal Building, Room 1310
300 Ala Moana Blvd.
Honolulu, HI 96850
(808) 546-7108

Illinois

Dirksen Building, Room 1322
219 South Dearborn Street
Chicago, IL 60604
(312) 353-5136

Indiana

46 East Ohio Street, Room 123
Indianapolis, IN 46204
(317) 269-7161 or 7162

Iowa

210 Walnut Street, Room 191
Des Moines, IA 50309
(515) 284-4546

Kansas

One-Twenty Building, Room 101
120 South Market Street
Wichita, KS 67202
(316) 267-6311, ext. 106
In Johnson and Wyandott Counties dial 374-5702

Kentucky

Federal Building
600 Federal Place
Louisville, KY 40202
(502) 582-5130

Louisiana

F. Edward Hebert Building
610 South Street, Room 103
New Orleans, LA 70130
(504) 589-2764

Maine

Federal Building, Room 611
Sewall Street & Western Avenue
Augusta, ME 04330
(207) 622-6171 ext. 269

Maryland

Garmatz Federal Building
101 W. Lombard Street
Baltimore, MD 21201
(202) 962-3822

1900 E. Street, N.W.
DC Metro Area, MD 20415
(202) 737-9616

Massachusetts

3 Center Plaza
Boston, MA 02108
(617) 223-2571

Michigan

477 Michigan Avenue, Room 595
Detroit, MI 48226
(313) 226-6950

Minnesota

Federal Building
Ft. Snelling, Twin Cities
Twin Cities, MN 55111
(612) 725-3355

Mississippi

100 W. Capitol Street, Suite 335
Jackson, MS 39201
(601) 490-4588

Missouri

Federal Building, Room 129
601 East 12th Street
Kansas City, MO 64106
(816) 374-5702

Federal Building, Room 1712
1520 Market Street
St. Louis, MO 63103
(314) 425-4285

Montana

Federal Building & Courthouse
301 S. Park, Room 153
Helena, MT 59601
(406) 449-5388

Nebraska

U.S. Courthouse and Post Office Building
Room 1014
215 N. 17th St.
Omaha, NE 68102
(402) 221-3815

Nevada

Mill & S. Virginia Streets
PO Box 3296
Reno, NV 89505
(702) 784-5535

New Hampshire

Federal Building, Room 104
Daniel & Penhallow Streets
Portsmouth, NH 03801
(603) 436-7720 ext. 762

New Jersey

Federal Building
970 Broad Street
Newark, NJ 07102
(201) 645-3673
In Camden, dial (215) 597-7440

New Mexico

Federal Building
421 Gold Avenue, S.W.
Albuquerque, NM 87102
(505) 766-2557

New York

590 Grand Concourse
Bronx, NY 10451
(212) 292-4666

111 W. Huron St.
Buffalo, NY 14202
(716) 846-4001

90-04 161st Street, Room 200
Jamaica, NY 11432
(212) 264-0422

Federal Building
26 Federal Plaza
New York City, NY 10278
(212) 264-0422

100 South Clinton Street
Syracuse, NY 13260
(315) 423-5660

North Carolina

Federal Building
310 New Bern Avenue
PO Box 25069
Raleigh, NC 27611
(919) 755-4361

North Dakota

Federal Building, Room 202
657 Second Avenue N.
Fargo, ND 58102
(701) 237-5771 ext. 363

Ohio

Federal Building
1240 E. 9th Street
Cleveland, OH 44199
(216) 522-4232

Federal Building, Lobby
200 W. 2nd Street
Dayton, OH 45402
(513) 225-2720 and 2854

Oklahoma

200 NW Fifth Street
Oklahoma City, OK 73102
(405) 231-4948

Oregon

Federal Building, Lobby (North)
1220 S.W. Third Street
Portland, OR 97204
(503) 221-3141

Pennsylvania

Federal Building, Room 168
Harrisburg, PA 17108
(717) 782-4494

Wm. J. Green, Jr.
Federal Building
600 Arch Street
Philadelphia, PA 19106
(215) 597-7440

Federal Building
1000 Liberty Avenue
Pittsburgh, PA 15222
(412) 644-2755

Puerto Rico

Federico Degetau Federal Building
Carlos E. Chardon Street
Hato Rey, P.R. 00918
(809) 753-4209 ext. 209

Rhode Island

Federal & Post Office Building, Room 310
Kennedy Plaza
Providence, RI 02903

South Carolina

Federal Building, Room 201
U.S. Court House
515 9th Street
Rapid City, SC 57701
(605) 348-2221

Tennessee

Federal Building
167 North Main Street
Memphis, TN 38103
(901) 521-3956

Texas

1100 Commerce Street, Room 1C42
Dallas, TX 75242
(214) 767-8035

Property Trust Building, Suite N302
2211 E. Missouri Ave.
El Paso, TX 79903
(915) 543-7425

701 San Jacinto Street
Houston, TX 77002
(713) 226-5501

643 E. Durango Blvd
San Antonio, TX 78205
(512) 229-6600

Utah

1234 South Main Street, 2nd Floor
Salt Lake City, UT 84101
(801) 524-5744

Vermont

Federal Building, Room 614
PO Box 489
Elmwood Ave & Pearl Street
Burlington, VT 05402
(801) 524-5744

Virginia

Federal Building, Room 220
200 Granby Mall
Norfolk, VA 23510
(804) 441-3355

1900 E Street, N.W.
D.C. Metro Area, VA 20415
(202) 737-9616

Washington

Federal Building
915 Second Avenue
Seattle, WA 98174
(206) 442-4365

West Virginia

Federal Building
500 Quarrier Street
Charleston, WV 25301
(304) 343-6181 ext. 226

Wisconsin

Plankinton Building, Room 205
161 West Wisconsin Ave
Milwaukee, WI 53203
(414) 244-3761

Wyoming

2120 Capitol Ave., Room 304
PO Box 967
Cheyenne, WY 82001
(307) 778-2220 ext. 2108

Paralegal Associations in the United States

National

American Academy of Legal Assistants
Professional Arts Building
1022 Park Avenue, N.E.
Norton, VA 24273

American Association for Paralegal Education
PO Box 40244
Overland Park, KS 66204

National Association of Legal
  Assistants, Inc.
PO Box 7587
Tulsa, OK 74105

National Federation of Paralegal
  Associations, Inc.
Ben Franklin Station
PO Box 14103
Washington, D.C. 20044

American Paralegal Association
PO Box 35233
Los Angeles, CA 74105

National Indian Paralegal
Association
7524 Major Avenue North
Brooklyn Park, MN 55443

Legal Assistant Management Association
PO Box 40129
Overland Park, KS 66204

National Paralegal Association
60 East State Street
Doylestown, PA 18901

Alaska

Alaska Legal Assistants Association
PO Box 13083
Phoenix, AZ 85002

Arizona

Arizona Paralegal Association
PO Box 13083
Phoenix, AZ 85002

Tucson Association of Legal
Assistants
PO Box 257
Tucson, AZ 85702

Northern Arizona Paralegal Association
Northern Arizona University
PO Box 7692
Flagstaff, AZ 86001

California

California Alliance of Paralegal Association
PO Box 26383
San Francisco, CA 94126

Orange County Paralegal
Association
PO Box 8512
Newport Beach, CA 92658

California Public Sector Paralegal Asociation
Stockton Street, Suite 400
San Francisco, CA 94133

Paralegal Association of
San Mateo County
250 Wheeler Avenue
Redwood City, CA 94061

Central Coast Legal Assistants Association
PO Box 1582
San Luis Obispo, CA 93406

Paralegal Association of Santa
Clara County
PO Box 26736
San Jose, CA 95159

Channel Cities Legal Assistants Association
PO Box 1260
Santa Barbara, CA 93120

Sacramento Association of Legal
Assistants
PO Box 453
Sacramento, CA 95802

East Bay Association of Legal Assistants
PO Box 424
Oakland, CA 94604

San Diego Association of Legal
Assistants
PO Box 12508
San Diego, CA 92112

Los Angeles Paralegal Association
PO Box 24350
Los Angeles, CA 90024

San Francisco Association of
Legal Assistants
PO Box 26668
San Francisco, CA 94126

Colorado

Legal Assistants of Colorado
PO Box 628
Gunnison, CO 81230

Rocky Mountain Legal Assistants
Association
PO Box 304
Denver, CO 81230

Connecticut

Connecticut Association of Paralegals
The Travelers Insurance Company
One Tower Square
Hartford, CT 06115

Greater Hartford Chapter
Connecticut Association of
Paralegals
PO Box 3594
Hartford, CT 06103

Connecticut Paralegal Association
PO Box 134
Bridgeport, CT 06604

Delaware

Delaware Paralegal Association
PO Box 1362
Wilmington, DE 19899

District of Columbia

National Capitol Area Paralegal Association
PO Box 19505
Washington, D.C. 20036

Florida

Broward County Paralegal Association
Ruden, Barnett, McCloskey, et al.
PO Box 1900
Ft. Lauderdale, FL 33302

Jacksonville Legal Assistants
PO Box 52264
Jacksonville, FL 32201

Florida Legal Assistants, Inc.
Director, Region Vll
4221 Cherry Laurel Dr
Pensacola, FL 32504

Georgia

Georgia Association of Legal Assistants
PO Box 1802
Atlanta, GA 30301

Hawaii

Hawaii Association of Legal Assistants
PO Box 674
Honolulu, HI 96809

Idaho

Boise Association of Lawyer's Assistants
PO Box 50
Boise, ID 83728

Illinois

Illinois Paralegal Association
PO Box 857
Chicago, IL 60690

Indiana

Indiana Legal Assistants
230 East Ohio Street
Sixth Floor
Indianapolis, IN 46204

Indianapolis Paralegal
  Association
PO Box 44518
Federal Station
Indianapolis, IN 46204

Iowa

Iowa Legal Assistants Association
PO Box 335
Des Moines, IA 50302

Paralegals of Iowa, Ltd.
3324 Kimball Ave
Waterloo, IA 50702

Kansas

Kansas Association of Legal Assistants
700 Fourth Financial Center
Wichita, KS 67202

Kentucky Paralegal Association
PO Box 34503
Louisville, KY 40232

Kansas Legal Assistants Society
1174 S.W. Filmore
Topeka, KS 66604

Louisville Association of
  Paralegals
PO Box 962
Louisville, KY 40201

Louisiana

New Orleans Paralegal Association
PO Box 30604
New Orleans, LA 70190

Maine

Maine Association of Paralegals
DTS PO Box 7554
Portland, ME 04111

Maine Paralegal Association
Union Mutual Life Insurance
2211 Congress Street
Portland, ME 04112

Maryland

Baltimore Association of Legal Assistants
PO Box 1653
Baltimore, MD 21203

Massachusetts

Berkshire Association for Paralegals &
  Legal Secretaries
Grinnell & Dubendorf
PO Box 576
Williamstown, MA 01267

Massachusetts Paralegal
  Association
PO Box 423
Boston, MA 02102

Michigan

Legal Assistant Association of Michigan
2477 Bratton
Bloomfield Hills, MI 48013

Michigan Association of Legal
  Assistants
17371 Collinson St.
East Detroit, MI 48201

Minnesota

Arrowhead Association of Legal Assistants
PO Box 221
Duluth, MN 55801

Minnesota Association of Legal
  Assistants
PO Box 15165
Minneapolis, MN 55415

Mississippi

Mississippi Association of Legal Assistants
PO Box 966
Jackson, MS 39205

Missouri

Kansas City Association of Legal Assistants
PO Box 13223
Kansas City, MO 64199

St. Louis Association of Legal
  Assistants
PO Box 8705
St. Louis, MO 63102

Nebraska

Nebraska Association of Legal Assistants
PO Box 81434
Lincoln, NE 68501

New Jersey

New Jersey Legal Assistants Association
Central Jersey Paralegal Division
PO Box 403, U.S. Hwy I30
Dayton, NJ 08810

New Jersey Paralegal Association
232 Inza Street
Highland Pk, NJ 08904

Paralegal Association of Central Jersey
93 Princeton Court
Mercerville, NJ 08021

South Jersey Paralegal
  Association
412 East Linden Ave.
Lindenwold, NJ 08021

New Mexico

Legal Assistants of New Mexico
PO Box 1945
Albuquerque, NM 87103

New York

Central New York Paralegal Association
Bond, Schoeneck & King
One Lincoln Center
Syracuse, NY 13202

New York City Paralegal Association
FDR Station, PO Box 5143
New York, NY 10022

Paralegal Association of
Rochester
700 Midtown Tower
Rochester, NY 14604

North Carolina

Cumberland County Paralegal Association
PO Box 1358
Fayetteville, NC 28302

Metrolina Paralegal Association
PO Box 32397
Charlotte, NC 28232

North Carolina Paralegal Association
PO Box 10214
Raleigh, NC 27605

Paralegal Association of Charlotte
1130 East Third Street
Charlotte, NC 28280

Raleigh-Wake Paralegal
Association
PO Box 10096
Raleigh, NC 27605

Triad Paralegal Association
Drawer U
Greensboro, NC 27402

Ohio

Akron Paralegal Association
3361 Boyne
Barberton, OH 44203

Cincinnati Paralegal Association
PO Box 1515
Cincinnati, OH 45201

Cleveland Association of Paralegals
PO Box 14011
Cleveland, OH 44144

Legal Assistants of Central Ohio
PO Box 15182
Columbus, OH 43216

Toledo Association of Legal
Assistants
PO Box 1842, Central Station
Toledo, OH 43612

Oregon

Oregon Legal Assistants Association
PO Box 8523
Portland, OR 97207

Willamette Valley Paralegals, Inc.
Bohemia, Inc.
2280 Oakmont Way
Eugene, OR 97401

Pennsylvania

Paralegal Association of N.W.
  Pennsylvania
PO Box 1504
Erie, PA 16507

Pennsylvania Paralegal Association
Central Susquehanna Valley Legal Services
142 Market Street
Sunbury, PA 17801

Philadelphia Association of
  Paralegals
PO Box 55
Philadelphia, PA 15230

Pittsburgh Paralegal Association
PO Box 1053
Pittsburgh, PA 15230

Rhode Island

Rhode Island Paralegal Association
PO Box 1003
Providence, RI 02903

South Carolina

Carolina Paralegal Association
7437 Highview Rd
Columbia, SC 29204

Tennessee

East Tennessee Association of Legal
  Assistants
3370 Jackson Circle, S.E.
Cleveland, TN 37311

East Tennessee Paralegal Association
450 Maclellan Building
Chattanooga, TN 37402

Mid-South Association of Legal
  Assistants
PO Box 3646
Memphis, TN 38103

Tennessee Valley Legal
  Assistants Associations
Stone & Hinds, P.C.
Suite 700, First American Center
507 Gay Street, S.W.
Knoxville, TN 37902

Texas

Alamo Area Professional Legal
  Assistants, Inc.
615 Soledad, Suite 300
San Antonio, TX 78205

Capitol Area Paralegal Association
PO Box 2353
Austin, TX 78768

Fort Worth Paralegal Association
PO Box 17021
Fort Worth, TX 76102

Houston Legal Assistants
  Association
PO Box 52241
Houston, TX 77052

Dallas Association of Legal Assistants
PO Box 50812
Dallas, TX 75250

El Paso Association of Legal Assistants
El Paso National Bank Bldg, 11th Floor
El Paso, TX 79901

Southeast Texas Association of
  Legal Assistants
725 Wade
Beaumont, TX 77706

Utah

Legal Assistants Association of Utah
Jones, Waldo, Holbrook, et al.
Walker Bank Building
Salt Lake City, UT 84111

Virginia

Central Virginia Legal Assistants Association
PO Box 4461
Lynchburg, VA 24502

Richmond Association of Legal
  Assistants
McGuire, Woods & Battle
One James Center
Richmond, VA 23219

Paralegal Association of Virginia
PO Box 1081
Emporia, VA 23847

Roanoke Valley Paralegal
  Association
Bird, Kinger and Huffman
126 Church Ave. S.W.
Roanoke, VA 24011

Public Service Paralegal Association
  of Virginia
PO Box 3922
Norfolk, VA 23514

Washington

Washington Legal Assistants Association
PO Box 2114
Seattle, WA 98111

Wisconsin

Paralegal Association of Wisconsin
PO Box 92882
Milwaukee, WI 53202

Local/National Newspapers, Legal and Non-Legal

- Classified advertisements

- News stories

- Position wanted ads

Professional Organizations

Job Fairs/Newsletters

- American Bar Association

- State and County Bar Associations

- Regional Paralegal Associations

College and Law School Placement Offices

Trade Associations

Political Organizations

Religious Organizations

Women's Organizations

Court House Bulletins

Chambers of Commerce

Libraries

Professional Journals, Legal and Non-Legal

Yellow Pages

Appendix B: Job Search Notebook, Checklists and Final Recommendations

This notebook offers a series of reminders to help you in the final stages of your job search. The checklists for each section serve to check the completion and accuracy of specific information. Final recommendations will add to the professionalism of your material.

Resumé Checklist

Appearance
- Color _____
- Weight _____

Format
- Production Choice
  Typeset _____
  Laser Printing _____

Quantity _____

Cost (per 100) _____

Due Dates _____
- Assignment date (if relevant) _____
- Printer delivery date _____

Content
- Accuracy (verification of names, dates) _____
- Editing (spelling, grammar, usage, style) _____
- Proofreading _____

Resumé

Portfolio of Writing Samples

The following guidelines will help you as you develop a portfolio of writing samples.

- Select the most appropriate examples of professional writing *you* have done at your job or as part of your coursework at school.

- Clearly identify the type or purpose of the writing sample (such as audience, assignment label, or length).

- Type all samples. Handwritten writing samples should be typed for your portfolio.

- Proofread each sample carefully to avoid spelling, grammatical, or typing errors.

- Choose works which are brief, focused, and achieve the purpose for which they were written. It is better to have shorter (1-2 page) samples and include greater variety.

- Avoid *personal* topics or controversial issues in selecting content areas.

- Have a former professor or respected colleague evaluate materials before including them in your portfolio.

- Do not violate confidentiality. If real names and events are referred to, delete or change details or request permission to use such information.

- Make certain all materials have a professional appearance. Class papers, reports, memos (or any other materials that have been circulated) should be clean copies.

Below are some types of writing that could serve as samples in your portfolio. They include school/work assignments and writings on your own initiative.

- A legal research memo or report
- A motion
- A set of interrogatories
- Answers to a set of interrogatories
- An index to discovery documents
- An appellate brief
- An intake memorandum of law

- An answer to a problem in the textbook
- A digest of one or more discovery documents
- Sample reports or studies

Ask teachers and supervisors to select samples which best represent your writing style. You may include remarks, comments, and grades if they provide a positive evaluation of your writing style.

References

The final line of your resumé indicates that references are available upon request. The following guidelines may help you to choose the most appropriate reference. Contact these references as soon as you begin your job search to obtain their permission to use their names. Finally, be certain to inform your references when you accept a position and to thank them in a letter for their help to you in your job search.

Types of References

- Generally three or four references are requested on a job application.

- The best references will be ones who know you and can genuinely support you for a position.

- Professional references may include: teachers, former employers, project directors, or professional colleagues.

- Professional references should be able to

  — Address your strengths, weaknesses, potential for growth
  — Vouch for your job performance and work habits
  — Comment on your personal/professional characteristics and qualifications such as reliability, initiative, commitment, integrity, and so forth.

- Personal references (if requested) should address your honesty, integrity, reputation within the community, and so forth.

- If you have limited job experience, rely on a reference who has seen your work either on a special project (part-time or volunteer) or in or out of class.

- Choose your references as they relate to the position for which you are applying.

  — Someone who knows you and your work in the legal field

— Someone who has observed you in a position that required the same or similar qualifications required of a paralegal (working with details, deadlines, clients, and so forth).

- Aim for a variety of references if you have limited work experience so that employer has verification of your abilities as well as capabilities.

Reminders

- Employers *will* check your references. So be certain to contact references for permission and to inform them about the job or jobs for which you will be applying so they can think about why you would be a good candidate.

- If writing to a reference for permission, identify how and in what context you know the person. For example, mention the class you attended, specific papers or projects you worked on, or any other details which could help the reference recall your specific qualifications.

- In requesting permission from a former boss or supervisor, refresh that person's memory (particularly if the job was not in the recent past) by recalling the specific dates of your employment and in what capacity you worked.

- If you are unable to contact a former employer or if you have reason to believe that you would not receive a favorable recommendation and if that job was a significant part of your work history, ask a former colleague who knows your work well to serve as a reference for that particular employment period.

First-hand observation of a job applicant is very useful to an employer. And if you remember that employers are looking for a person with the *personal* as well as *professional* qualifications, you will choose references who can comment on both aspects. Remember that employers are looking for someone who will fit into the organization and be able to get along with the other employees.

Finally, references can and should be a valuable asset to your job search. Do not take them for granted. Always extend to them professional courtesies by contacting them for permission before you apply for the job and after you accept a position to let them know the results of your search.

Job Sources Checklist

- Friends/relatives in paralegal/legal profession _____
- Teachers _____
- Colleagues/former colleagues _____
- Former employers _____
- Alumni associations _____
- Community/civic associations _____
- Job fairs _____
- Job directories _____
- Legal secretaries _____
- Legal administrators _____
- General directories of attorneys _____
- Special directories of attorneys _____
- Placement offices _____
  - —Colleges/universities _____
  - —Local law schools _____
- Government job listings _____
- Newspapers and newsletters _____
  - —Want ads/general circulation of daily papers _____
  - —Legal newspapers _____
  - —Paralegal newsletters _____
- Bulletins of all civic/community/professional organizations _____
- Professional associations _____
  - —Paralegal associations _____
  - —Business/management associations _____
  - —Specialty fields associations _____
  - —Employment agencies _____

Letters Checklist

Type of letter	Sent to:/Date	Response received/Date (if appropriate)
Reference request (may be a telephone request)	_____	_____
	_____	_____
	_____	_____
Acknowledgement letter	_____	_____
	_____	_____
	_____	_____
Cover letter	_____	_____
	_____	_____
	_____	_____
	_____	_____
	_____	_____
	_____	_____
	_____	_____
Follow-up letter	_____	_____
	_____	_____
	_____	_____
	_____	_____
	_____	_____
	_____	_____
	_____	_____
	_____	_____
Job acceptance	_____	_____

Interview Checklist (For personal/job information preparation)

- Specific job/position _____
- Organization/firm _____
- Location _____
- Time of interview _____
- Name of interviewer _____
- Transportation:
  —Public (time schedule) _____
  —Auto (parking facilities) _____
  —Confirmed directions _____
- Departure time _____
- Arrival time _____
- Dress code _____
- Resumé copies _____
- Writing samples portfolio _____

Information on Position

- Employer specialty _____
- Duties/responsibilities of paralegal position _____
- Required training, experience, education _____
- Supervisory structure _____
- Methods of supervision _____
- Support staff (such as clerical) _____
- Client contact _____
- Career opportunities _____
- Performance evaluation _____
- Continuing education: Required _____
  Support _____   Reimbursement _____
- Billable hours expected of paralegals _____
- Travel _____
- Overtime _____
- Compensation/benefits (salary, bonus, health plan, life insurance, sick leave, vacation, maternity leave, parking, and so forth)
- Decision deadline

Interview Self-Evaluation Checklist

(May be used for each job interview)

Position/Organization   Date   Positive/Negative Evaluation of Position/Interview

_____ _____ _____

_____ _____ _____

_____ _____ _____

I would/would not like this position _____

I was/was not satisfied with the interview _____

Difficult questions asked _____

_____

_____

Self-evaluation of responses _____

_____

Improved responses   _____
(for next interview) _____

_____

_____

Follow-up   Letter(s) sent _____

Letter/response received _____

Second interview _____

Interview results

Job offered _____   Job not offered _____

Accepted _____

Declined _____   Reasons: _____

Accepted _____   _____

Starting date _____

Salary_____

Benefits _____

_____

_____

Paralegal Specialties

The following listing of paralegal specialties reflects the growing trend for paralegals to specialize. Many paralegals develop specialties in several areas because of the overlapping of duties and responsibilities in these areas. Within each category a brief description of the major paralegal functions with the specialty is included. Duties and responsibilities may vary with the position. For more information and details, consult a firm, organization, or agency that handles the specific specialty that interests you. In all areas, of course, the paralegal works with or for an attorney.

Administrative Law

Government positions that handle citizen queries and complaints and draft proposed regulations and statutes for agencies. Positions also available with law firms that represent citizens before particular agencies (U.S. Patent Office, Welfare Department, and so forth).

Paralegal duties include: investigation, research, advocacy at agency hearings, drafting pleadings for litigation, attending hearings, and preparing reports, exhibits, or witnesses.

Admiralty Law

Law covering accidents, injuries, and deaths connected with vessels on navigable waters. Paralegal duties include: investigation, research, and litigation assistance.

Antitrust Law

Paralegal work includes aspects of document control (pleadings, deposition testimony, interrogatories, and exhibits); indexing documents, drafting pleadings, investigation (statistical data and corporate structures); legal research on monopolies, marked allocation, or the Federal Trade Commission Act.

Banking Law

Paralegal assists legal staff in such tasks as assessing bank liability for negligence claims, collection abuse, and claims. Assists attorneys in litigating claims, monitors activities of various banking regulatory agencies, drafts and reviews loan applications and credit documents. May also analyze documents (mortgages or security agreements), arrange closings, prepare notarization of documents, monitor recordation, and conduct Uniform Commercial Code (UCC) searches.

Bankruptcy Law

Paralegal interviews clients on matters of bankruptcy; reviews questionnaires on assets and liabilities. Investigates indebtedness, verifies tax liabilities, identifies creditor claims. Arranges for asset valuation, prepares inventories of assets/liabilities, and opens bankruptcy petitions and answers creditor inquiries.

Change of Name Law

Paralegal researches, gathers records, and drafts applications, files applications and pleadings in court on behalf of individuals and organizations requesting name change.

Law of Children

Paralegal works with attorney in all aspects of investigation, preliminary draftings, client counseling, legal research and litigation assistance in cases involving adoption, child abuse, custody, paternity, and juvenile delinquency. See also Domestic Relations.

Civil Rights Law

Assists in litigation brought by citizens or law firms representing citizens in discrimination complaints, including complaints based on sex, race, religion, or age.

Commercial Law Collections

Paralegal investigates claims, conducts asset checks, verifies information. Litigation assistant in Civil Court and Small Claims Court.

Communication Law

Government paralegal assists attorneys in Federal Communications Commission (FCC) work of regulating the communications industry. Assists in litigation and representation of citizens or companies in drafting applications for licenses; prepares compliance reports, exemption applications, and statistical analyses.

Construction Claims

Paralegal works with engineering consultant claims including data collection, graph preparation, document preparation, and arranging for arbitration of claims.

Consumer Law

Specialty includes all aspects of consumer problems and public or private concerns that affect them: utility shut-offs, garnished wages, default judgments, lost credit cards, automobile insurance suspension, merchandise complaints, defective goods, unsatisfactory repair work, insurance claims, and so forth.

Paralegals investigate, draft forms and reports, counsel clients, and assist in litigation. They also help citizens in case preparations before Small Claims Court, train other paralegals to handle consumer cases, educate community groups on consumer laws, and draft consumer-education reports.

Contract Law

All aspects of law of contracts included in this specialty: antitrust law, banking law, bankruptcy law, construction law, construction claims, corporate law, copyright law, domestic-relations law, employee-benefits law, employment law, government-contract law, insurance law, international law, landlord-tenant law, oil and gas law, partnership law, real estate law, tax law, and so forth.

Paralegal duties include investigation of alleged breach of contract, legal research on law of specific contracts, litigation assistance in trial of breach of contract case, and preparation of form contracts.

Copyright law

Paralegals assist clients in copyright registration, collect data for applications, file applications, prepare contracts, investigate any existing infringements, and assist in general litigation. Patent law and trademark law are related specialties.

Corporate Law

This specialty includes incorporation and corporate work: drafting preincorporation subscriptions, recording Articles of Incorporation, preparing documents, attending directors' meetings and drafting minutes, drafting sections of annual reports, general document preparation, legal research for documents on pending legislation, preparing case profiles, monitoring law journals or newspapers, maintaining corporate forms file, and assisting in processing patent, copyright, and trademark applications.

Criminal Law

Paralegal works for prosecutors with: case reviews, police liaison, citizen complaints, consumer fraud, nonsupport and Uniform Reciprocal Enforcement of Support Act (URESA), and bad-checks restitution. Serves as Calendaring Aide to Calendar Court, witness liaison and in trial preparation.

Paralegal works for defense attorneys with: arranging for bail, determination of eligibility, diversion, initial client review, planning community services for clients, liaison with detained defendants, fieldwork assistance, trial preparations, plea negotiations, and appeals and collateral attacks.

Domestic Relations Law

Paralegal works with attorney in problem identification and resolution in domestic issues (divorce, law of children, and so forth). Conducts preliminary interviews, consults with lawyers, drafts complaints and summons, judgment, and separation agreement; acts as general litigation assistant and trains other staff.

Education Law

The field includes issues concerning school board procedures or citizen advocacy. Paralegal conducts preliminary interviews with parent or child, identifies nonlegal problems for referral to other agencies, serves as an informal advocate, appears at school board meetings, before legislative committees, attends formal hearings representing child, counsels clients, and assists in litigation.

Employee-Benefits Law (Qualified Plans)

Paralegal works closely with attorney, plan sponsor, administrator, and trustee in preparation and drafting of qualified employee plans. Prepares accompanying documents and monitors program, handles government compliance work, prepares and reviews annual reports of plan.

Employment Law

Paralegal identifies and investigates problems concerning individual complaints based on discrimination, demotion (or failure to promote) due to discrimination, and alleged nonpayment of salary. Prepares documents for hearing, serves as an informal advocate and negotiations mediator. Related to Labor Law and Civil Rights Law.

Government Contract Law

Paralegal maintains calendar for Courts and Appeals Board, prepares claims and documents for appearing and post-hearing brief in matters concerning government contracts.

Health Law

Paralegal consults with attorney in problem identification and resolution in all aspects of legal health issues. Investigates medical records, visits sites to explore public health issues, may serve as interpreter of foreign language between medical staff and patient (explaining hospital procedures), addresses community groups on health law issues, serves as informal advocate, and in negotiation mediation. Appears before legislative committees or health administrative bodies to express views on health-care issues.

Immigration Law

Paralegal identifies immigration problems, including difficulties in obtaining visa, permanent residency difficulties, nonimmigrant status, citizenship status, deportation proceedings. Provides information on visa process, residency, registration process, citizenship process, and deportation process. Assists individuals in obtaining documents, refers individuals to foreign consulates or nationality organizations for assistance. Helps individuals in completing all required forms.

Insurance Law

Paralegal duties involve legal research, processing disputed benefit claims, assisting in litigation on claims brought to court, monitoring activities of insurance regulatory agencies and committees of the legislature with jurisdiction over insurance. Related to Employment Benefits Law.

International Law

Paralegal researches, prepares, and/or coordinates documents and/or data regarding international trade, for presentation to the Commerce Department, Court of International Trade, or other governmental bodies.

Labor Law

Paralegal investigates and examines documents, assists in litigation in labor disputes before Labor Relations Board, State Labor Relations Board and the courts. Drafts documents, arranges for depositions, prepares statistical data, appeals, and exhibits. Relates to Employment Benefits Law, Unemployment Compensation Law, and Worker's Compensation Law.

Landlord-Tenant Law

This field includes issues relating to public and private housing. Paralegal files application for procedures, conducts preliminary interviews, drafts orders or letters requesting hearings, and serves pleadings on landlords.

Law Office Administration

Paralegal manages/supervises all aspects of personnel and office procedures. Evaluates performances, oversees accounting functions, establishes procedures for billing verification, supervises law library, establishes and maintains filing system, administers insurance programs for firm, prepares long-range budget projections, prepares reports of individual attorneys and departments within the firm.

Legislation

Paralegal monitors all events, persons, and organizations involved in passing of legislation relevant to client of firm. Drafts proposed legislation, prepares reports/studies on the subject of proposed legislation.

Litigation

Paralegal investigates, performs document research, discovery, files/serves; assists in trial preparation, in client preparation, including arranging client interviews, expert witnesses, supervising document encodation. Assists in preparation of trial briefs, appeal documents, and other legal research.

Lobbying

Paralegal works with lobbying attorneys in research of legislative, regulatory history, monitors proposed regulations of administrative agencies and of the legislature.

Military Law

Paralegal assists in document preparation for military proceedings, claims against the government, court reporting, and maintenance of all records.

Motor Vehicle Law

Issues concerning license suspension or revocation are the focus of this law. Paralegal assists clients in gathering records, serves as informal advocate for client with Department of Motor Vehicles, assists client in preparation of case before hearing officer in suspension/revocation of license cases.

Oil and Gas Law

Paralegal collects, analyzes data pertaining to land ownership and activities affecting procurement of rights to explore or drill for and produce oil or gas. Helps to acquire leases and monitors execution of leases and other agreements; helps to negotiate agreements, processes and monitors termination of leases and agreements, examines land titles. See also Real Estate Law.

Parajudge

In states where judges in certain lower courts are not required to be an attorney (local magistrates court, Justice of the Peace courts), paralegals may have limited roles in conducting designated pretrial proceedings and making recommendations to regular court.

Partnership Law

Paralegal drafts pre-organization agreement, records minutes of meetings and agreements for dissolution of partnership. Drafts and publishes notice of termination of partnership, drafts noncompetitive agreements for selling partners, and assignment of partnership interests.

Patent Law

Paralegal helps inventor apply for a patent with the U.S. Patent and Trademark Office, conducts patent search, monitors responses from government offices, helps market invention by identifying licenses, studies market, prepares contracts, and investigates patent infringements.

Post-Conviction and Corrections Law

Paralegal works with inmate who wishes to appeal conviction and helps to identify problems. Helps with all aspects of appeal, including writing administrative complaints and gathering relevant records.

Real Estate Law

Paralegal assists law firms, corporations, development companies in transactions involving land, houses, office buildings, condominiums, shopping malls, and so forth, with research in zoning regulations, title work, mortgage closings, checking with compliance on all disclosure settlements, foreclosures, office management, and tax-exempt industrial development financing.

Tax Law

Paralegal compiles all data for preparation of tax returns (including corporate income, employer quarterly, franchise, partnership, sales, personal property, individual income, estate, gift); drafts extensions, maintains tax-law library, and compiles supporting documents for returns.

Tort Law

Paralegal mainly provides litigation assistance in civil wrong that has injured someone: negligence, trespassing, defamation, strict liability, wrongful death and, frequently, worker's compensation cases for on-the-job injuries.

Trademark Law

Paralegal researches documents, investigates, prepares foreign trademark applications, maintains files, responds to official government actions, and investigates trademark infringement. See also Copyright Law.

Tribal Law

Paralegal assists in civil and criminal cases in which both parties are Native Americans. Drafts and files complaints, presents written and oral appeals to tribal court of appeals.

Trusts, Estates, and Probate Law

Paralegal collects data, handles preliminary drafting of will or trusts and investment analysis in estate planning. Manages office, assists in estate of decedent (including assets phase, accounting phase, and termination-distribution phase). Assists in general litigation, including: preparing sample pleadings, legal research, preparing drafts of interrogatories and notarizing documents.

Unemployment Insurance (Compensation)

Paralegal meets with clients, investigates and solicits affidavits from employers, handles time determinations, serves as informal advocate with both parties, represents clients before Unemployment Insurance hearing examiner. Counsels clients, presents petitions before legislative and administrative hearings, and addresses community groups.

Welfare Law

Paralegal holds preliminary interviews to explain welfare issues, meets with welfare department, investigates and verifies information, conducts hearings and follow-up with hearing attorney. Assists attorney in gathering documents for appeal, files papers in court, and serves papers. Trains other paralegals and speaks to community organizations.

Worker's Compensation Law

Paralegal interviews claimants, collects data, drafts claims, requests hearings, and serves as formal/informal advocate. Follows up to determine whether payment is in compliance with awards, monitors claims, and files statutory demand for proper payment, if necessary.

Index

S